HACKERCRAFT

James P. Barry

MBI Publishing Company

Dedication
For Anne

First published in 2002 by MBI Publishing Company, Galtier Plaza, Suite 200, 380 Jackson Street, St. Paul, MN 55101-3885 USA

MBI Publishing Company books are also available at discounts in bulk quantity for industrial or sales-promotional use. For details write to Special Sales Manager at Motorbooks International Wholesalers & Distributors, Galtier Plaza, Suite 200, 380 Jackson Street, St. Paul, MN 55101-3885 USA.

Library of Congress Cataloging-in-Publication Data available

ISBN 0-7603-1107-2

Edited by: Paul Johnson
Designed by: Dan Perry

Printed in China

On the front cover: *Shooting Star*, a restored 28-foot Hackercraft from 1938 is shown at speed. *Classic Boating*

Endpaper: This 19-foot Hackercraft was an example of the smaller utility designs that became popular after World War II. *From a Hacker Boat Company Catalog*

On the frontispiece: This detail depicts the logo from Hacker's ultimate streamliner, *Thunderbird*, a 55-footer replete with art deco details. *Classic Boating*

On the title page: A 1922 Hacker "Peerless" racing runabout. *Classic Boating*

On the back cover: *Eagles' Nest,* a restored Hacker runabout of uncertain date. shows a good turn of speed. *Classic Boating* Despite world-altering events like the Great Depression and World War II, Hackercraft continued to offer standard runabouts like this 32-foot model from 1931. © *Mystic Seaport, Rosenfeld Collection, Mystic, Connecticut*

Contents

Acknowledgments

Many people have provided the material for this book. Marion Hacker Hurst contributed her own recollections, allowed me to read Hacker family papers, and provided photographs. Tom Flood gave his wealth of Hacker information; supplied copies of catalogs, photographs, and other material; read sections of the book in draft; and was always available to answer questions. S. Steven McCready furnished Hacker Boat Company records, commented on them, read chapter two in draft, and contributed

photographs. Ronald Lane provided information about Hacker cruisers and the Hacker-Fermann relationship. Bill Morgan discussed Hacker's designs and his own.

Phil Bolger, Jay Ottinger, and Nelson Zimmer recalled their contacts with John L. Hacker. Don MacKerer provided the extracts from letters written by his father. Tom Netschke provided Hacker family memories. F. Todd Warner furnished copies of his Hackercraft catalogs and other publications.

William Campbell guided me through sources of racing information, and his racing scrapbooks were invaluable. Greg Calkins, researcher and bibliographer of boat racing, provided much early information, especially in the Pacific Coast area. L. K. Muller and Bob Senior provided material on the ultimate Hacker racers, *My Sweetie* and *Miss Pepsi*. Paul Miklos gave information about the Century company and its boats at the time of the Hackers' connection. Joseph Gribbons provided early guidance and encouragement.

Robert Murnan of the Cleveland Research Center and Ruth McMahon, Detroit genealogist, made major contributions. C. Patrick Labadie let me use his file of *Sail and Sweep* magazine. Stephanie Chontos of the Ford Research and Access Center provided copies of correspondence between Edsel Ford and John L. Hacker. Phoebe B. Tritton of the Antique Boat Museum located information and photographs. John Polacsek of the Dossin Great Lakes Museum, Detroit, gave guidance, photographs, and information about the Dossins' *Miss Pepsi*.

John W. Pemberton of the Mariners' Museum, Virginia Sharps of the Rosenfeld Collection at Mystic Seaport, Peggy Tate Smith of Mystic Seaport, and Jim Wangard of *Classic Boating* spent much effort helping me obtain photographs. Many other staff members at the Mariners' Museum and at Mystic Seaport helped to find information.

The interest and enthusiasm of Jim Wangard and Jack Savage moved the book project forward in many ways. Thanks also are due Jack Savage for reading the book in manuscript and providing expert guidance.

Bow of *Thunderbird* showing some of her art deco details. *Classic Boating*

Introduction

John L. Hacker was born to design and build boats. Despite repeated interruptions to his career that would have caused other men to change occupations, he continued on. From early youth until his death, he seems to have been driven by the overwhelming need to make boats.

And what boats! He designed winning racers throughout his life. His artistic eye was unparalleled. It is seen most clearly in his beautiful stock Hackercraft, for which he still is best known. But oddly—the prerogative of a genius, perhaps—toward the end of his life he was proudest of the many handsome cruisers that he had designed during his long and productive career.

Starting at the age of 14, when he was a schoolboy in Detroit putting together a rowboat, and possibly climaxing at age 74, designing a 94-foot crash rescue boat for the U.S. Air Force, boats were his life. Often they took precedence over his family, whom he expected to adjust to his comings and goings, his curious schedules, and his emotional ups and downs.

In some ways he seemed to be a typical self-made man; he sometimes spoke ungrammatically, and he doggedly wore his brown business suits on the most formal occasions. Yet he associated easily with the affluent and well-educated people who commissioned him to design their boats, and if he did not like the boat they wanted he told them to go elsewhere.

His Hackercraft runabouts were fast-moving works of sculpture, works that were frequently copied by his competitors. Because of their elegant construction and finish, they often were called the Steinways of boats. They not only were beautiful, they rode well in the water and were supremely seaworthy. His runabouts were exported to much of the world and his designs were sent out to be used by distant builders. There was, for example, the boat design that he sent to Manila for H. L. Heath and that was "built by two Chinamen." He was the most influential pleasure boat designer of his day—the day of wooden power-boats. We know that his work was copied widely by other American builders, but there is no record of its effect on builders in the more than 100 countries where there were people with whom he corresponded.

Until the boom period of the late 1920s, the Hacker Boat Company offered only one or two runabout models at a time and completed about three boats a week. In 1928 the company began to expand, but soon encountered the Great Depression of the early 1930s, which considerably diminished it. Hackercraft were never built in large numbers. At some regattas there would be special races for Chris-Craft or for Dodge Watercars, yet there never were races for Hackercraft alone—there just were not enough of them. But Hackercraft often were entered in open races for runabouts, and they often won.

John Hacker started in the American motor boat business at its beginnings. He led the way in design and in excellence of construction for most of his life. At the time of his death at age 84, he was still designing boats, just as wooden boats were passing. Appropriately, the modern revival of interest in such boats has been led by a company that has also revived his name.

Rebel, a 1924 custom 33-foot Hacker, one of two built. *Classic Boating*

Hacker's *Kitty Hawk II* is pictured in 1911 with its initial Van Blerck engine of 100 horsepower. That year it won a challenge race in Atlantic City for the 26-foot championship, which brought it to national attention. It was the first boat to reach 50 miles per hour. A later owner put in a 150-horsepower Van Blerck. In a Chicago race in 1912, traveling at about 50 miles per hour, it caught fire and sank. *The Mariners' Museum, Newport News, Virginia*

Chapter One

A Passion for Design

John Hacker's Legendary Career Begins

As the nineteenth century rolled into the twentieth, Detroit was the technical center of North America. It was a place that attracted bright young minds. It was a place of bubbling ideas, of young men who wanted to do new things with the old knowledge, who moved from company to company, and who wanted to set up their own firms. It was the equivalent in those days of what today we call Silicon Valley.

The main focus of the place was the development and use of the internal combustion engine. The most obvious use was in automobiles, but Detroit had its own river, a busy waterway between two Great Lakes, and boats provided another obvious place to put engines. Boats had the further advantage of not being hindered by the poor roads of the day or by speed limits.

If Detroit was attracting young engineering geniuses from all over the country, it lay at the feet of a talented young man who was born and went to school there, who had an unceasing drive to design and build boats, and whose abilities in time made him the foremost artist-designer of powered wooden craft. His name was John L. Hacker.

John Ludwig Hacker, the first of 11 children of Johann F. and Marie Machris Haacker, was born in Detroit on May 24, 1877. On August 12 he was baptized Johann Ludwig Haacker in the German-speaking Trinity Lutheran Church. Among the sponsors was Ludwig Haacker, possibly the baby's grandfather. Before long the first names of both father and son were anglicized to John, and the second *a* disappeared from the family name.

The parents were established Detroiters; Marie Machris was born there to one of the old French families; John F. was brought there from Buffalo when he was a child. In 1889 John F., who first worked as a cabinetmaker and patternmaker, built a store that had living quarters above it. A barn behind the store held machinery that John F. had invented and patented, which stamped and gummed ballot slips that were used all over

the country. Changes in voting methods ended this work, and he went on to the ice and coal business. The elder Hacker was a solid citizen of Detroit. In 1895, as the Republican candidate in a thoroughly Democratic ward, he won the office of alderman. He won again in 1898. Soon after the new century began, when the city charter was revised, he became a member of the revision committee.

When the young John L. was 12 years old, his piano teacher wanted him to become a professional musician. An unidentified music organization offered to pay his parents $75 a month while it trained him, but his parents refused. Growing up, after his daily classes—first in a German Lutheran school for six years, then in the Detroit Public Schools—he spent his time along the waterfront, fascinated by the small boats there. He completed building his first one at the age of 14. He must have been a thoughtful young man who could work with figures, for a bit later he was employed as a bookkeeper at his father's business. While he worked there, he took correspondence courses and attended night school to learn naval architecture, the art and science of boat design. At the age of 21, he joined the Masonic Order and in 1919 he became a 32nd Degree Mason.

Young Hacker's surroundings at the turn of the century were the normal ones of the time. Women no longer wore bustles, though their skirts still touched the ground. The drawings of the slim Gibson Girl, by the popular artist Charles Dana Gibson, were the ideal; they often showed her holding a tennis racket. The West had largely been won, but Buffalo Bill's Wild West Show still brought city dwellers a whiff of cowboys-and-Indians gunsmoke. In the cities, only the relatively affluent could own a horse and carriage. Nearly everyone rode the electric streetcars—a condition that Detroit would one day change.

Steam drove the power plants that generated the electricity. Steam drove factory machinery. Steam drove large ships and small workboats such as tugs. The basic power of

A Hacker runabout of the early 1900s, *Go Devil* was typical of her day. The long forward deck over the engine and the canvas top followed the pattern of early automobiles. *The Mariners' Museum, Newport News, Virginia*

the time was provided by steam engines. But steam launches used for pleasure were rare in the United States because any steam plant there had to be operated by a licensed engineer who had served two years as a stoker before taking his examination. Even people who had some money thought it hardly worthwhile to employ an engineer to run a small craft.

But then the patented naphtha engine appeared. Naphtha was an early form of gasoline. The naphtha engine used the stuff both as the fuel under the boiler and the expanding fluid in the boiler—it boiled gasoline. The expanding gas was fed into an engine not unlike the later internal-combustion engine. It had small cylinders, often three of them, which drove a crankshaft, which in turn drove the propeller shaft. It bypassed the regulations on steam engines, and required no licensed engineer to run it. An early experimenter with a naphtha engine was Christopher Columbus Smith of nearby Algonac, Michigan, who later would give his name to Chris-Craft.

By the time the regulatory agencies woke up to how the naphtha engine was spreading, the internal-

combustion engine—sometimes referred to as the gasoline explosive engine—was also coming along. The regulators wanted authority to control both naphtha and internal-combustion engines as they did steam engines, and they set up a board to study the matter. *Sail and Sweep*, a Detroit-based boating magazine, in its issue of October 1903 described the situation under the heading "LAUNCH MEN UP IN ARMS." At the end of its full-column article, it summarized in this way:

"Already launch owners in all parts of the country have been getting their protests in shape to present to the congressmen when they meet again. The objections will not only come from the owners of these pleasure craft, but from manufacturers as well. Such a law as has been proposed would greatly diminish, it is believed, the demand for small vessels of this kind, so the establishments that put them on the market are much stirred up over the matter.

"The opinion of the members of the board is that such legislation would be wise and would be another safeguard around water traffic."

Luckily, the members of the board lost.

"VAN BLERCK" IN THE LEAD.

John L. Hacker and Henry Ford each worked to perfect a form of moving vehicle powered by an internal combustion engine. They patronized the same machine shops in Detroit and came to know each other. They remained friends until Ford, who was 14 years the elder, died. Hacker also rubbed elbows with, and probably knew, many of those who worked with Ford and shortly would be the automotive giants of the day—men such as Alfred P. Sloan Jr., a salesman of roller bearings who would eventually become head of General Motors; Henry Leland, who was starting Oldsmobile and would go on to Cadillac; and the Dodge Brothers, whose machine shop built some of Ford's early chassis. The Dodges would become automotive titans, and one brother's son, Horace Jr., whose eventual five marriages would keep the tabloids happy, would also grow to be a vigorous member of the boat-racing circle that drew in Hacker. So would Ford's son, Edsel.

In 1902 Hacker married Bertha Schrank. In 1905 their son, John A. Hacker, was born, followed by daughters Marion, in 1911, and Eleanor, in 1915. In naming its sons, the family seemed almost intent on confounding historians—three generations of John Hackers, differentiated only by the middle initials, F., L., and A.

Au Revoir, 1903

John L. Hacker made a considerable advance toward becoming a professional designer and builder of boats in 1903, when he constructed *Au Revoir*, a boat of his own design, for Willard Murray Smith of Detroit. It was a long, thin craft, 32 feet 6 inches in length, 4 feet 6 inches in beam, which drew 8 inches loaded. *Au Revoir* won local races for money—reaching 23 miles per hour over a 20-mile course with what is variously described as a 55-horsepower Speedway motor and a 100-horsepower Seabury. *Au Revoir* repeatedly beat 75-footers designed by Herreshoff, the noted East Coast naval architecture and building firm, and attracted national attention. As the October 10, 1904, issue of *Motor Boat* magazine described it, "The hull is very flat and has a sharp run forward for about 18 feet. The forward deck is 9 feet long with a 5 inch sweep, turtle effect." The writer concluded, "When her length is considered, she is probably the fastest boat of her size and power in this country."

Sail and Sweep described the boat in this way: "Her keel is 2 x 5, ribs 1/2 x 1, with 8-inch centers, both of white oak. She is planked and decked with 7/16-inch clear British Columbia red cedar. Her interior finish is of quartered white oak 7/8-inch thick, finished in malachite green, with red moldings and upholstery. Her steering gear is an auto wheel, which is placed directly aft of the motor or in the center of the boat, which has a limit of six passengers."

The position of the wheel enabled one person both to steer the boat and look after the engine, in a day when engines still needed much cosseting. It had a transom that in profile sloped backward from the after gunwale to the water, thus increasing its length on the waterline. Its propeller shaft projected a foot or so behind its transom, so that the propeller was behind the boat, and so was the rudder. Its characteristics led *Sail and Sweep* to make the comment, more thoughtful than critical, that "The entire hull is of peculiar design."

In 1906 Hacker built two fast commuters—26-foot cabin boats—for lumbermen who lived on Lake St. Clair and wanted to travel by water to their Detroit offices, at a time when roads were still minimal and rail schedules inconvenient. These boats were the predecessors of the striking high-speed cruiser-commuters that would later come from his drawing board.

The Hacker Boat Company, 1908

In 1908, John L. took the major step of going fully into business on his own. He bought the Detroit Launch & Power Company, said to have been a failing concern, renamed it the Hacker Boat Company, and went vigorously to work. (His father may have been a silent partner.) That first year he built a racer named *Van Blerck*. When it was put in the water it refused to plane. Investigating, he found that in lofting the design, the sides of the boat had been raised 9 inches. Carelessness or sabotage? Careless *over*-building of a boat seemed unlikely. In those days there was hot competition between racers, which usually had

large bets placed on them, and sabotage on the part of a worker was suspected. In the future, Hacker was careful to supervise more closely the construction of his boats. *Van Blerck* was rebuilt and later became a competent racer.

He hit upon a more notable design with *Gretchen,* said to be the first hydroplane with a bow rudder. The innovation came through desperation. Hacker is quoted as saying, "She would not plane with conventional rudders aft. With rudders removed and throttles used for steering she planed perfectly. The bow rudder was tried and with success."

During the next three years, Hacker built perhaps 30 boats. Sometimes he is credited with initiating the idea of stock boats about this time, but boat advertisements as early as 1903

say "on hand" or "always in stock." It was an idea whose time had come, and no doubt many had it. Probably none of them—not even Hacker—at that time devoted their main effort to stock production (that is, boats built in anticipation of buyers, rather than on contract for particular buyers).

Even in those early years, Hacker was not limited to small craft. In 1910 and 1911 he produced two 44-foot cruisers, a 50-foot tug, and an early raised-deck cruiser (a pattern that would become widely used in later years) named *Advance.*

In October 1911 Hacker installed two floats of his own design and construction on a Wright Brothers biplane, so the plane could take off and land on water. This probably was the first use of twin floats on an aircraft.

Here is *Kitty Hawk Jr.* in 1913. In the Toledo, Ohio, regatta that year it made a time and stamina record by running a total of 90 miles—in several races—in a total of 2 hours, 14 minutes, and 14 seconds. © *Mystic Seaport, Rosenfeld Collection, Mystic, Connecticut*

Kitty Hawk II, 1911

In 1911 Hacker built *Kitty Hawk II,* the first 50-mile-per-hour boat in the United States, which during the following season was the fastest boat around Detroit, winning every race for its type. Then in 1911 it raced *Baby Reliance* in St. Louis. *Baby Reliance* was a noted boat designed by Christopher Columbus Smith, the rising boat designer and builder of Algonac, Michigan. Smith's boat had won almost every race she entered. There were to be three heats, one a day. On the first day, *Baby Reliance* won. During the second heat, *Kitty Hawk II* was well in the lead when *Reliance* stopped dead on the course. It had been agreed in advance that if one of the boats was unable to finish the course, the race was off. When the spectators, who had heavily bet on the race, discovered this agreement, there followed what one writer called a "rhubarb." No further description of the rhubarb was given.

In September 1911 *Kitty Hawk II* defeated a boat called *Sand Burr II* in a challenge race at the latter's native Atlantic City. Hacker's boat won, giving it, according to *Motor Boat,* claim to "the 26-foot championship of the country." *Sand Burr II* had engine problems, while *Kitty Hawk II* ran well, covering 24 miles in 46 minutes, 9 4/5 seconds. Many East Coast yachtsmen had dismissed Midwestern (usually written off by the generic term "Western") boats as unworthy of serious attention. *Kitty Hawk II's* performance in Eastern waters began to change that attitude—but in mid-August 1912, at the Chicago Regatta, "while traveling close to 50 miles an hour, she caught fire and sank about 1 1/2 miles from shore."

Breakdown

In 1911, with success drawing within reach, Hacker suffered a breakdown. On his doctor's suggestion he took a vacation, stepped out of the company, and sold it. Having taken over a failing firm, he evidently worked himself to the point of collapse keeping it afloat, even with its successes.

During 1912 and 1913 he advertised as a freelance designer from time to time among the small business cards published at the back of the boating magazines:

JOHN L. HACKER, N.A.
Hydroplane and SpeedCraft a Specialty
Designer of "Kitty Hawk II"—the Fastest boat in the world for power; Speed 50:42 miles. Speeds guaranteed *Cor. Hubbard and Jefferson Aves., Detroit, Mich.*

After the sale of his company he also began to do boat designs for one of the leading marine-engine builders in the country, Joseph Van Blerck.

Back in 1909 Joe Van Blerck, an immigrant from Holland, had been running a small engine-building shop in Detroit. His engines were well known and well regarded by powerboat builders in the area. He was designer, builder, and office manager. At some point Charles E. Page, a Cleveland businessman, joined him and set up a new plant, located at Monroe, Michigan, half way between the city of Detroit and Lake Erie. A branch of the Detroit River, the River Raisin led to the Van Blerck dock. Boats would come to have

their engines overhauled or new engines installed. Page took over the office workings, which didn't suit Van Blerck's interests or abilities. (It was well known that Van Blerck was not an office man; a report in the August 1914 *Motor Boat* asked, "Can you imagine Joe Van Blerck swearing into a Dictaphone!")

Operating with Van Blerck was a boatbuilder named S. A. Ferris. It was not unusual then for marine engine builders also to build boats. In 1914 Ferris built the Hacker-designed *Hawk Eye* at the Van Blerck shop and Van Blerck installed a 12-cylinder engine of his own design and construction. The hull design was that of an

improved *Kitty Hawk*. Other *Kitty Hawks* followed over the next few years—*Kitty Hawk Jr., Kitty Hawk IV,* and *Kitty Hawk V*—all with Van Blerck engines.

In 1912 Hacker designed a boat that was vastly different from his racers. It displays his virtuosity, but perhaps also indicates that at that time he would do any kind of design to have some money in pocket. It was a 30-foot raised deck, round bottomed cruiser for Alex Fisher of Detroit. Plans for the boat, complete with its lines, appeared in the December 10 *Motor Boat*. Fisher may have insisted on the round bottom, for almost all of Hacker's boats had either V-bottoms or planing bottoms. "As a whole, this little craft is very pleasing,

A Buffalo entry in the 1914 Gold Cup race, the Hacker-designed *Buffalo Enquirer*, powered by a Sterling Engine made in Buffalo, was second in a field of 10. © *Mystic Seaport, Rosenfeld Collection, Mystic, Connecticut*

has proven an able sea boat, has sufficient port light and skylights for perfect ventilation, and makes a speed of 9 miles an hour with her 10-horsepower motor on long runs," the magazine commented. Hacker did a good job, even on a round-bottomed craft of a type he did not favor.

Oregon Kid, 1913

In 1913 he designed a racing hydroplane of which Gar wood is quoted as saying "We never had a real hydroplane until Hacker brought out *Oregon Kid.*" It was intended for use on the West Coast. *Pacific Motor Boat* of August 1913 described it:

"The *Oregon Kid* is a wonderful little 20-footer of the one-step hydroplane type, designed by John Hacker of Detroit, Michigan, who evolved the *Vamoose* of the Pacific Coast and the *Kitty Hawks* of the East last year. She is equipped with the same engine that was used in the *Vamoose,* a 100-horsepower six-cylinder 5 1/2 x 6-inch Van Blerck, which since last season has been sent back to the factory, overhauled and slightly improved, which has added considerably to its efficiency."

At the Pacific Coast Championship Races at Astoria that year it carried off the honors in the free-for-all race and in the 20- and 26-foot classes. It went on to wipe out all opponents at Seattle.

Oregon Kid was owned and built to Hacker's plans by Captain Milton Smith, owner of a fleet of tugboats on the Columbia River. He had built and raced the Hacker-designed *Vamoose* the preceding season, with mild success but not the honors that he wanted. The old *Vamoose,* with a new engine, was renamed *Van Blerck* and continued to campaign under that name. (That boat was far enough away in time and location that it was not confused with Hacker's earlier boat of the same name.)

With new owners, both *Van Blerck* and *Oregon Kid* were sent to race in the Midwest. The *Kid* won in regattas at Chicago and at Keokuck, where the *Van Blerck* capsized and went to the bottom. The owners surrendered it—as it lay on the bottom—to the insurance company. It was not heard of again. The *Kid* went on to compete at Buffalo. There, in the middle of a free-for-all race on the Niagara River, it hit a big wave, turned over, and sank. For some reason, it remained on the bottom for eight days before it was recovered. It went on to compete

at Kansas City and at Louisville, with poor performances at each place. The long submersion at Buffalo put an end to its career. It was shipped home, but did not compete again.

Oregon Kid II appeared on the Pacific Coast in 1914. "*Oregon Kid II* is owned by the same owners, built by the same builders and in fact as is nearly an exact duplicate to the *Oregon Kid* as it was possible to make her." It was driven by a six-cylinder Van Blerck of slightly later model and slightly more horsepower. At Astoria that year it was raced by two teenaged men, one of them a son of Captain Smith, who built and owned it. It won the 20-foot Coast Championship. It also won the free-for-all, but less gloriously, as all of its opponents either were disqualified or fell out for one reason or another.

In April 1922 *Motor Boating* published a Hacker design that provides a good sense of the *Oregon Kid.* The piece was part of a series that the magazine presented on up-to-date boats that readers could have builders make for them. *Motor Boating*

published the complete plans, including all specifications needed to build a small hydroplane, and offered blue prints at nominal cost. It headlined the material, "This Fast Hydroplane is Patterned After the Famous Oregon Kid Which Established Many Records in Its Day."

The piece said, "This little boat was only 20 feet in length and was, in a large measure, the forerunner of our present hydroplanes." The magazine's new design increased the length by 2 feet, but no other changes were described. The boat had a single step in a boxy hull that displayed some tumble home aft. The first third of the boat was covered by a deck with a moderate crown; the rest was open with narrow side decks until, at the stern, a patch of deck covered the gasoline tank, "a 16 by 30-inch seamless steel tank." Squeezed in between the engine and the gas tank was the crew's space, with a bench for two people and an automobile-type steering wheel for the driver. Side planking was to be 7/16-inch mahogany or cedar. (No doubt the original *Kid* was planked in

The Albany Boat Company, where Hacker worked for about a year, with a boat of Hacker's design in the foreground.
The Mariners' Museum, Newport News, Virginia

cedar, before mahogany became usual.) Bottom planking was double, the inner layer of 3/16 inch, laid diagonally, the outer of 3/8 inch laid fore and aft.

Construction was light. "Much attention has been paid to the reduction in unnecessary weights. With high speed craft, each pound counts. The light materials must be carefully handled and assembled in order to secure the greatest benefit from their lesser weight."

The engine of the new boat stood just aft of midships. It was not boxed in, but stood importantly, visible well above the gunwales. "The exhaust will be disposed of through short stacks attached to the exhaust ports in the machine." We can visualize the *Oregon Kid* as a small, light, single-step hydroplane with a large engine standing tall in the cockpit, and with short stacks for the exhaust.

The Move to Albany

As World War I began in Europe and the storm threatened to spread, John Hacker was approached by the Japanese Navy. The Japanese had spent five years studying some 5,000 fast boat types around the world and had settled on Hacker to design a PT boat for them. Hacker, though the offer was flattering, steered clear of international complications and refused to do the job.

In 1914 the Hacker 30-foot displacement (today it would be called a semidisplacement) runabout *Stroller*, with a six-cylinder 100-horsepower Van Blerck, cleaned up at Albany. Designed by Hacker and built by the Albany Boat Company, it beat *Elmer II*, the former champion of the upper Hudson River, and soon afterward defeated Vincent Astor's new 55-footer.

A Van Blerck engine promotional booklet published about 1914 lists all the winning Hacker boats at that time that had Van Blerck engines. In addition to *Stroller* there were *Kitty Hawk I, Kitty Hawk Jr., Kitty Hawk II, Kitty Hawk IV,* and *Kitty Hawk V.* The booklet also mentioned *Oregon Kid* and perhaps the most exotic, *Cloverleaf,* called

"Asiatic Champion." Designed by Hacker, powered by Van Blerck, this boat was "owned by Mr. H. L. Heath of Manila and built by two Chinamen."

In February 1915 a young journeyman boatbuilder, A. W. MacKerer, wrote to his mother:

". . . am now in Detroit, working in a first-class boatshop. Have a good chance here on high speed racing boats and must say it is dandy work. Hacker Boat Co. is about 4 miles from Detroit and is only a small but fine place. Detroit you know is the city of automobiles and is certainly a pretty place. Fred [Cahill—his foreman] and I live with the Hackers right over the shop and certainly get treated fine. Six dollars a week for room, eats and washing. I can use them for references anytime I feel like. They are holding down orders for boats, and are going to start again in about six months. They are building nothing but engines and I could work on that if I wanted to, but I want to learn all about my trade and don't want to waste my time at anything else, if possible."

Hacker never was known as an engine builder and his work here is puzzling. Perhaps his old friend Van Blerck was helping him out by giving him some employment. Evidently Hacker was also doing some boat work; otherwise he would not have hired MacKerer. But in July the work ran out. MacKerer was one of four boatbuilders who would be retained, though his efforts and pay were limited to five hours a day. He decided to move on.

Clearly Hacker was not unduly prosperous. Later that year he joined L. L. Tripp, Van Blerck's eastern sales agent, in Tripp's Albany Boat Company, located near that city, in Watervliet, New York. While Hacker was chief designer there, the Albany Company's boats changed from round-bottom launches to hard-chine V-bottom boats. After about a year at Watervliet, John Hacker had another breakdown. The reasons are not clear. The Albany Boat Company was a large concern, and his responsibilities may have weighed heavily on him. It has been suggested that he had disagreements with Tripp. In any event he disappeared into a sanitarium, where he stayed for some time. The location of the sanitarium and the length of his stay are uncertain.

Hydroplanes and V-Bottoms, 1915–1921

In contrast with John Hacker, who worked out his designs on his drawing board, the other rising designer of the period, Christopher Columbus Smith, whittled out half models from which he built his boats. The difference was striking, but both produced winners. In 1915 Smith's *Miss Detroit* won the Gold Cup—the ultimate North American powerboat trophy—under the most embarrassing circumstances imaginable, when every other boat in the contest, including Hacker's *Hawk Eye,* fell out because of mechanical troubles.

Then in 1916 the millionaire Gar Wood arrived on the Detroit scene and joined forces with Smith. Wood's design philosophy was simple: put the most powerful engine possible in a boat and see how fast it would go. With unlimited power (and nearly unlimited money) his boats would dominate Gold Cup contests through the 1921 race, after which the American Powerboat Association, tiring of Wood's one-man shows, changed the rules. Competing boats could no longer be hydroplanes. Their engines had to have limited power. In general, they had to be of more reasonable and useful types. Usually they were V-bottomed. Other designers again competed. (Wood, however, continued to race his monster hydroplanes successfully in international contests.)

John Hacker was as strong an advocate for the V-bottom in most pleasure boats as he was for the planing bottom in unlimited racers. In an introduction to one of his designs he wrote, "Professional builders prefer the more conventional round bottom type as offering less difficulties in the shop. The V-bottom type, however, has so many advantages to offset the slightly increased amount of work necessary to produce it that these are not permitted to weigh against it."

The V-bottom grew out of earlier patterns. The first powerboats were displacement craft, pushing their way through the water. As boats developed, a hull shape that we now call semidisplacement evolved. It had a sharp bow that ran back to an almost flat bottom. At relatively slow speeds it pushed its way along, just like the older displacement boats. But if a powerful engine drove it fast enough, the flat bottom would plane, lifting much of the craft above the surface and thus cutting down the friction between boat and water. Such boats were sometimes referred to as monoplanes—they planed on a single surface—before the name was applied to aircraft.

This form could be built either following the type of traditional boat that had round bilges, or with a V-bottom. The latter inherited its shape from two earlier traditions. Its bow had the sharp entry of some of the later displacement boats that had been built like knives on edge, long and thin, cutting their way through. Such boats had comparatively deep V-bottoms that would not plane. The newer shape added toward the stern the

flat bottoms of dories or sharpies. The side of such a boat meets the bottom at a distinct angle; the line where they join is the chine.

Boats with V-bottoms, especially boats of smaller sizes, can be driven faster more easily than boats with round bottoms. Today there still are arguments as to whether round-bottom hulls are more seaworthy in rough weather, and as to how large a V-bottom hull can be built practically. But for Hacker's purposes the V-bottom was obviously best, and most builders of fast pleasure boats soon followed his example.

Development of the Runabout Form

During his time at Watervliet, Hacker no doubt came into closer contact with another thread of powerboat development, about which he must already have known a good deal. It began some years previously and came from the Thousand Islands area of the upper St. Lawrence River, just east of Lake Ontario.

The first two Gold Cup races were run in 1904 on the Hudson River at New York City.

Then for the next nine years they were won by dueling autoboats, as they then were called, belonging to yacht clubs in the Thousand Islands, and as a result the races were always held there. During that decade, the racing boats developed rapidly from displacement craft to planing craft.

The Thousand Islands was a summer resort area that attracted well-to-do families. Summer residents, surrounded by water, in close association with the racing autoboats, wanted boats of their own. The many boatbuilders in the area, most of whom produced racers for the Gold Cup, could easily turn out less exotic craft. The tie between cars and powerboats that would become so evident after Detroit developed into the major auto center was already close, and so the automotive term "runabout," used for a sporty car, was also adopted for a small, nimble boat.

The word "runabout" in nautical usage then did not have its later connotations of glistening mahogany and chrome, engines under hatches, and passengers in airplanelike cockpits. The early runabouts took whatever form the buyers and

builders decided. The most usual was a semiopen boat with a long forward deck, under which rode the engine. The influence of the powerful cars of the day with their long hoods probably encouraged the use of forward decks that sometimes were exceptionally long.

Hacker was struck by the distance between the driver of such a boat and the bow, because the faster the boat moved, the more the helmsman needed good visibility. Yet as the boat moved faster, its bow rose, limiting visibility from the stern. And the water thrown up by the bow tended to reach, and sometimes temporarily blind, people in the aft area, while a forward cockpit was clear of it. He became an advocate of the forward cockpit.

But like many innovators, he actually made popular an idea that others had before him. In *The Rudder* for April 1909, there is a plan for a two-cockpit runabout, with controls in the front cockpit (the engine is even farther forward), designed by B. B. Crowninshield, who was better known as a designer of sailboats. And even the Crowninshield boat was not hailed as a new form. Hacker was probably aware of all this. He called himself a pioneer in the use of the front cockpit, but never its inventor.

While he was at Watervliet he designed a V-bottom 32-footer for use on Lake George. It apparently was built in 1916. He moved the engine to a midship location and installed a cockpit containing the controls forward of it. This was a move toward what became the classic runabout type. For a time, such a boat might retain, aft of its engine, an open passenger space containing wicker chairs, but gradually that area also became a decked-in cockpit.

As with many innovations, the forward controls were not immediately popular. For some time, shiny mahogany runabouts were built in which the aft passenger space became a cockpit with the controls located there, and no forward cockpit. Boats were also built that had forward cockpits but retained the controls at the stern. Hacker himself continued to design and build many of these variations, probably because the customers wanted them. Racing boats at the time carried their two-man crews at the very stern, just aft of engines that required careful tending, and that arrangement would remain normal among racers for years to come. No doubt owners of runabouts used for racing also wanted the controls aft. Others probably felt that they looked sportier if their boats followed suit. But eventually it became standard practice for a runabout to have the controls forward. Hacker remained the leader in this, as in most features of runabout design.

Starting Again

Back in Detroit, always tenacious and needing to exercise his talent, he again started the Hacker Boat Company, at 321 Crane Avenue. The exact date is uncertain. One of his standard 25-footers (with stern cockpit and controls) was sold to the technical editor of *Automobile* magazine. The boat traveled at 20 miles per hour, powered by a four-cylinder Scripps motor, and had electric starting and lighting.

In 1916 he enjoyed learning that his old *Hawk Eye* still was going strong and had won the Thousand Islands Cup on the upper St. Lawrence River. In 1917 he produced the racing hull of *Miss Miami* for airplane manufacturer Glen Curtiss; the boat became the platform for an experimental marine installation of a Curtiss 350-horsepower airplane engine, reaching the speed of 67 miles per hour. The next year that same engine, further honed by Gar Wood, went into Wood's *Miss Detroit III,* which easily won the Gold Cup. Hacker, despite his work on *Miss Miami,* remained an advocate of marine engines designed specifically for watercraft, rather than supporting the converted airplane engines that Gar Wood made popular in his early years of racing.

In 1919 a Hacker-designed boat, *Eleventh Hour,* competed for the Gold Cup. On the second lap, *Eleventh Hour* was closing steadily on *Miss Detroit III* and seemed poised to take the lead when it was hit by a wave and swamped. Even so, Hacker's boat ran the fastest heat of the race at 50.4 miles per hour. (No one ever said that the fastest racers were seaworthy.)

The First Bear Cats, 1918

In the fall of 1918 Hacker designed and built six runabouts. Three were sold to E. W. Gregory of the Belle Isle Boat and Engine Company and became the earliest Belle Isle Bear Cats. Another went to a Chicago owner who named it *N'Everythin',* and used it for racing. Boats went to J.W. Packard of

the Packard Motor Company and to Edsel Ford. One went to the silent movie star Dustin Farnum, whose name had national recognition. With it he won the Nordlinger Trophy on the West Coast. He came back several times for a new Hacker boat, and with each continued to win Pacific Coast contests.

Hacker considered one of his 1918 boats, named *Dough Boy,* to be the first stock runabout with forward controls.

The next fall Hacker sold four of his 26-foot standard runabout hulls to Belle Isle. These apparently had their controls in forward cockpits. One of them, powered with a six-cylinder Hall-Scott engine, was shipped off to California to B. C. Scott, president of Hall-Scott, where the runabout performed sensationally, easily doing 40 miles per hour. The manager of the Belle Isle Company, Ed Gregory, fitted the remaining ones with four-cylinder Hall Scotts, and sold them as Belle Isle Bear Cats. (Again the auto tie-in was evident; the name was copied from the Stutz Bear Cat cars, then the dashing equivalent of today's sports cars.) About this time Hacker began to advertise that he "pioneered the forward cockpit runabout."

Hacker's reputation as a designer of runabouts was settled. He soon would become the most influential runabout designer-builder among the three leading builders. The other two were Smith and Wood, who in time separated and became competitors.

In September 1919 *Motor Boating* ran a full-page picture feature headed "One May Truly Run about in These Runabouts Powered with Sterling Motors and Designed by John L. Hacker Whose Reputation as a Designer of Speedy Craft Dubs Him a Real 'Craftsman.'" The strained cleverness of the heading may have set some readers' teeth on edge, but the meaning was clear.

One photo caption under this heading said, "*Cure II* is a 26-foot runabout with a beam of 6 feet 6 inches, equipped with a Sterling Model FS motor, which maintains 33 miles per hour. She has repeatedly defeated every other four-cylinder craft on the Detroit River, and a great many of the sixes. Strasburg [her owner] is usually seen with a foot in each of the starboard and port bucket seats, standing up over the wheel, with the motor turning at 1,500 rpm looking for a race."

A 30-foot double-cockpit boat controlled from the rear cockpit was also pictured, but the third entry was the one that emphasized the designer's versatility. This boat, a 40-foot express

cruiser named *Condor*, had been built by Ditchburn, of Gravenhurst on the Muskoka Lakes, for Harry Greening, the Canadian sportsman and race driver. Powered by a Model FS eight-cylinder counter-balanced crankshaft type Sterling, it had reached 28 miles per hour.

That November the magazine printed a lengthy discussion as to whether hydroplanes were spoiling the sport of boat racing. As an example of a fast nonhydroplane, the article cited Hacker's *N'Everthin'*, a "displacement runabout"—actually the boat was what came to be called a "semi-displacement craft"—that had run at a speed "of 36 miles an hour for 10 miles," and "we believe it could show 40 miles an hour on a straightaway."

Hacker's Growing Fame

In December 1919 the young journeyman boatbuilder A. W. MacKerer, who had come back from World War I and was looking for a job, wrote home:

"Well, it is Detroit for mine, thank the Lord for that. I am going to work for Hacker. He wouldn't let me leave the shop until I promised to work for him. Hacker is going to fix me up with a place to live. I am glad to get this, for working for Hacker means a great deal in our business."

In March 1920 *Motor Boating* published a report on the New York Boat Show. The first page was given over to two boat pictures, one of them

"A Hacker 35-footer built for the Fisher Trophy Race and powered with two Hall-Scott marine motors. The whole outfit represents the highest degree of perfection ever reached."

Hacker's growing prominence led to a commission that further demonstrated his versatility, showing that he was able to design less flashy boats. *The Rudder* in November 1920 published plans of a more modest 40-foot V-bottom cruiser of his design, a double-cabin boat—with a trunk cabin forward rather than a raised deck—which could reach 12 1/2 miles per hour with a Kermath Model 40 engine. It was built for J. B. Farr of the Kermath Manufacturing Company. Kermath also bought the design, the blueprints of which it gave free to anyone who purchased a 40-horsepower Kermath to put in the boat.

By 1920, Hacker could afford full-page advertisements in the boating magazines. He was probably the first person to advertise stock runabouts of what today we think of as the classic type. One ad in December was headed by what would become a famous trademark, a script HackerCraft. But before describing the stock boats, it led off by saying, "Dustin Farnum's *ELEDA* a Hacker-built 31-Footer, Liberty powered, wins the NORDLINGER TROPHY, in three straight heats, at Los Angeles, Calif., in very rough water. *MISS LOS ANGELES*, also HACKER-BUILT won same race in three straight heats in 1919."

The glory years were starting for John L. Hacker.

The runabout *Canny Scot* around 1919. Hacker's eye for graceful design is already evident in the sheer line and the tumble home aft. *The Mariners' Museum, Newport News, Virginia*

Edward II, a 30-foot Hackercraft of 1930. It originally was owned by actor Edward Everett Horton, who kept the boat for some 40 years. Powered by a Sterling Petrel engine of 225 horsepower, it has been fully restored. *Classic Boating*

Chapter Two

Speed, Elegance, and Excellence
Hacker's Innovative Stock Boats

Hacker's association with the Belle Isle Boat Company continued. By 1920 Ed Gregory of that company was claiming publicly that Belle Isle designed and built its Belle Isle Bear Cat itself, but the runabout looked suspiciously like a Hacker boat. The controls were in a single forward cockpit. Aft of the engine was a large open space, which usually contained some wicker chairs. The design of the Bear Cat did not change greatly over the first few years. Perhaps it was a Hacker boat with a different nameplate, and Hacker was considered part of their team. Gregory managed the operation, but the actual builders at Belle Isle were Joe Pouliot and his son Russ, who would be associated with various Detroit boat concerns for many years, and would in time build some of Hacker's cruisers.

Or perhaps this was an early example of someone else poaching a Hacker design—in the following years Hacker boats were so widely plagiarized it became a standard joke that every time Hacker produced a new runabout his competitors bought one in order to copy it. Probably not many builders actually did that, but almost all of them borrowed his ideas.

Whatever the arrangement between Hacker and Gregory, it is clear that in this case any copying was with Hacker's consent.

The Hacker Boat Company—the best known company of several that had that name—was founded on March 26, 1920. In 1919 Hacker had purchased a lot in Mount Clemens, Michigan, and as early as January 1920, the company was advertising that its office was at 323 Crane Avenue, Detroit, and that it had factories both in Detroit and in Mount Clemens. That year a cement block building was erected for the company in Mount Clemens. Hacker was president; Paul Strasburg, one of his faithful customers who may have put some money into the company, was vice president; and a Hugh F. Palmer was secretary and treasurer.

The 40–Mile-Per-Hour Boat, 1920

In the 1920s, Hacker's full-page advertisements promoted the Hacker Boat Company, its address given variously as 321 Crane Ave., 323 Crane Ave., or 325 Crane Ave., in Detroit. Each displayed the now-familiar script trademark of HackerCraft. In February 1920 the advertisement announced:

"The 40-mile-Per-Hour Displacement Boat Is an Actual Fact. The sweet combination of Hacker Boat and Hall-Scott Motor does the trick. We are building for stock ten 29' 3" boats: some have already been sold. These we absolutely guarantee to make 37 mph or better. You may have one of these superboats for early delivery if you order early."

An April advertisement that year did not describe any specific boat. It announced that the company produced runabouts exclusively, and in one corner also noted that Hacker offered stock plans for sale. In addition it gave two names, "John L. Hacker, N.A., and Hugh F. Palmer, General Manager." In May the company returned to advertising the specific 40-mile-per-hour model, a full page announcing, "THE HACKER BOAT CO. Are the First Purveyors of ACTUAL 40-Mile-Per-Hour Displacement Boats." These boats were powered by six-cylinder Hall-Scott Motors, "if one wants the greatest speed efficiency"; otherwise four-cylinder Hall-Scotts would do "if one is satisfied with 33 mph or better."

Edsel Ford bought one of the latest Hacker 29-foot runabouts, which he named *Sialia Jr.* It was one of the 40-mile-an-hour specials with some minor modifications, according to the July 10 *Motor Boat,* so it was John L. Hacker's "latest creation." (Although these were standard boats they were not mass produced, and each one could be a little different.) *Sialia* had a small forward cockpit, but the controls were at the stern. Built of selected mahogany, with fastenings of bronze and copper, it was powered by the six-cylinder Hall-Scott, "which appeals particularly to Mr. Ford because

of his technical knowledge and experience with motor development, despite the difference between the high-powered marine motor and that which makes the Flivver go."

Edsel said that the car in which he drove to the boatyard was the three-millionth chassis turned out by his company and that in May the Ford plant had produced the four-millionth chassis. "John Hacker remarked that while the Hacker Boat Co. had scarcely reached such production in building motor boats, the output of the Hacker shops was increasing rapidly."

The 21-Foot Runabout, 1920

By December 1920 the Hacker advertisements offered both the 29-foot special and a 21-foot standardized runabout, "An absolutely high class outfit, completely equipped, speed 16 to 18 miles." Hacker now appealed to two markets—one seeking a comparatively large, fast, two-cockpit boat, and one a smaller, more modest runabout which had only an aft cockpit. (The latter would help carry him through the recession of 1921–1922.) The December ad also said, "Hacker Stock Plans: Special Plans will be made to your

order by John L. Hacker N.A., for any high class job up to 60 feet. Please write your requirement."

Hacker joined with William Fermann in 1922, forming a company that was to build cruisers on a custom basis and to act as yacht brokers—an operation completely apart from the Hacker Boat Company. Hacker was the designer, though custom boats that he produced during that time carried the label of Hacker & Fermann.

In 1922 Chris Smith and Sons set up a company separate from Gar Wood, with whom they had worked for some years, and began to advertise 24-, 26-, and 33-foot boats. They also still built 33-footers for Wood, who sold them as Baby Gars. Gradually Wood moved away from dependence on the Smiths and began to build his own boats, becoming a strong presence in the market for fast runabouts. Smith, whose mass-produced boats became Chris-Craft, and Wood, whose output was limited but whose name was widely known because of his racing prowess, plus Hacker, gradually became the three best-known builders of runabouts.

There were numerous others who turned out varying quantities of the boats—Dodge,

This is one of Hacker's two-cockpit runabouts with controls in the aft cockpit. These boats, which had six-cylinder Hall-Scott engines, were advertised as the first stock boats to go 40 miles per hour. He sold one to Edsel Ford in 1920. *The Mariners' Museum, Newport News, Virginia*

Race for Belle Isle Bear Cats, Detroit, 1921. Hacker's first stock runabouts with controls in forward cockpits were sold as Bear Cats by the Belle Isle Boat Company, which retained his designs for several years. These are typical of his early forward-control boats; there were no windshields and the space aft of the engine was not yet a true cockpit, but a place to carry wicker chairs on quieter days. Most had 100-horsepower to 125-horsepower Hall-Scott engines. Note the one boat with aft cockpit only. © *Mystic Seaport, Rosenfeld Collection, Mystic, Connecticut*

owned by racing enthusiast Horace Dodge Jr., was possibly the next best known—but it became commonplace to say that Chris-Craft produced the Fords, Gar Wood the Buicks, and Hacker the Packards of runabouts. (Packard in those days in North America was the equivalent of Mercedes in Europe.)

The similarities between Hacker's runabouts and the Belle Isle Bear Cats lingered and again became apparent during the Buffalo Regatta in September of 1923. In a runabout race the Hacker boat *June* won. The *Belle Isle Bear Cat* (racing under that name) came in second. Both boats were 26 feet long and had 6 feet, 6 inches beam; *June*

was powered by a 100-horsepower Hall-Scott, *Bear Cat* by a 125-horsepower Hall-Scott.

(In the racing class during that same regatta, the Hacker-designed and built *Baby June*—which had the same owner as plain *June*—won a narrowly contested race in which the Hacker-designed *Miss Mary* was close behind, actually winning two of the three heats but failing to show up for a third. *Miss Mary* would later become famous under a new name, *El Lagarto*.)

Hacker announced in December 1923 that he would enlarge the cement-block building he now had in Mount Clemens, and move his entire operation there.

Ballahoo was a 1922 Hacker runabout owned by Robert Wood Johnson of Johnson & Johnson, the medical supply company. Probably the boat was meant to be driven from the front cockpit by a nautical chauffeur while the family rode in the large rear cockpit behind the wood-framed windshield. © *Mystic Seaport, Rosenfeld Collection, Mystic, Connecticut*

The 24-Foot Dolphin, 1924–1925

In 1924 Hacker joined with the Belle Isle Boat & Engine Company to form the Belle Isle-Hacker Boat Sales Company, which marketed both Hacker and Belle Isle stock boats. The Bear Cat was produced in a single size, 26 feet long, with a hull that had not been changed since 1921. The Dolphin was now 24 feet long and was one of the first boats to have a forward cockpit, where the controls were located, that was enlarged so that it would accommodate six people on two upholstered bench seats. It had a windshield—Hacker was among the first to install them. The aft cockpit had become small, as it would remain in what became the classic form of a runabout.

A full-page advertisement for the Hacker Dolphin in the April 10, 1925, *Motor Boat* praised it as "A perfectly appointed all-purpose runabout. . . . Powered with the 90-horse Scripps marine motor." The Dolphin actually was offered with a variety of engines that would drive it at speeds ranging from 23 to 33 miles per hour, the most powerful being a Peerless 125-horsepower installation. There was a slightly raised box over its engines, which would gradually shrink and then disappear from later Hacker runabouts.

In smaller print at the bottom of the page was added, "The Belle Isle Super Bear Cat is a larger craft with even greater speed—accepted everywhere as the finest runabout built." Such an ad leads to further suspicion that Hacker had also designed the Bear Cats. (The name "Bear Cat" was often written as a single word, "Bearcat").

Richardson Boats, 1924–1925

In addition to his other work, Hacker designed runabouts for the Richardson Boat Company of North Tonawanda, New York, a Buffalo suburb. In 1924 Richardson offered a 20-foot rear cockpit boat and in 1925 a 25-footer, both of Hacker's design. The 20-footer was driven by an F-6 Scripps, the 25-footer by a D-4 Scripps. Both were stock boats that would compete with his own products. Perhaps in those early days he felt that Richardson was so far away that their sales areas did not overlap; perhaps the money paid at the time for the designs was more important than any theoretical future competition. In addition, he designed a custom 25-foot runabout, powered by an F-4 Scripps, with forward cockpit and controls for a Richardson customer who wanted a boat to use on Lake Champlain.

An Expanded Mount Clemens Plant

By 1925 the enlarged Hacker plant in Mount Clemens was turning out three Dolphins a week, according to an article in the May 25 *Motor Boat*. Over at Chris-Craft, A. W. MacKerer—who some years ago had improved his skills while working for Hacker—was factory superintendent and was setting up its first production line. On March 21, 1926, he wrote, "Started our first boat in the new plant today. In a week we will be going full blast with about 100 men on the payroll. In about a month we will be building 2 boats a day. Imagine thinking such a thing possible a few years ago." At Chris-Craft there was a separate milling department that cut boat parts by template and fed them to the work floor, where uniform Chris-Crafts were assembled. Until the Hacker plant was further expanded in 1928, it could not have greatly exceeded its three stock boats a week. (In addition it was making racers and other custom boats.) The total Chris-Craft yearly production by then was 830 boats.

One potential advantage to customers of Hacker's limited production was that he was able to build many of the boats as semicustom. Within reason, modifications could be made to the standard designs if someone wanted a boat that was a little different. As a result a number of almost-stock boats were constructed that did not exactly fit any overall pattern.

Gar Wood boats, the third of the industry leaders, did not build its own hulls until 1925, but in 1929 it produced 217 stock boats. In 1930, after moving into a new factory, it produced 193. Perhaps the slight reduction was a signal of the oncoming depression.

Hacker's expanded plant had been financed by C. P. McCready, who in 1925 installed his son S. Dudley McCready as secretary and treasurer of the company. The entrance of the McCreadys was vital. By providing a solid business framework to support Hacker's artistry, they kept this company from having the short life of all his other companies. The details of Hacker's agreements with them are not known, but in 1925 S. Dudley McCready wrote a reproving letter to Hacker, saying that in violation of the contract between him and the McCreadys, Hacker was having a Gold Cup boat built by the Belle Isle Boat Co. as a result of "certain personal financial difficulties."

The letter said that this time they would permit the boat to be completed at Belle Isle "with the distinct understanding that the Belle Isle Boat Company's name shall in no way be connected with this boat . . . and that the Hacker Boat Company shall receive the benefit of any success it may have."

What the personal financial difficulties were we do not know, but the incident reinforces the belief that Hacker was often in debt.

The incident may also have chilled relations between Belle Isle and Hackercraft. In early 1926 the Belle Isle-Hacker sales combination disappeared. The Hacker & Fermann Company—Hacker's separate organization to produce cruisers and act as yacht brokers—took over the distribution of Hacker runabouts. Whether the McCready letter had anything to do with the change we do not know. Perhaps the Fermann connection needed further reinforcement.

Stock Cruiser Designs, 1925–1926

Hacker's agreement with the McCreadys permitted him to design cruisers, which he did frequently. They were more often custom designs than stock boats, but the Hacker Boat Company did not build cruisers, so Hacker was able to prepare stock designs for other builders who wanted them. In 1925 he designed a handsome 40-footer for the Liggett Boat Company of nearby Wyandotte, Michigan, which quickly received orders from local yachtsmen for boats of that model. The design was normal for 1925 but looks odd today. Its bridge deck, instead of being an enclosed pilothouse–living room combination, had a fixed top but was open at the sides. There were comfortable staterooms under the raised deck forward and the trunk cabin aft, so that four

This is a 1924 Hacker 24-foot Dolphin. There is a windshield in front of the double cockpit, which has moved forward, leaving a small stern cockpit. This was one of the first stock boats to have the classic runabout form. The most powerful engine fitted was a 125-horsepower Scripps that drove the boat at 33 miles per hour. *Courtesy Tom Flood*

could live very comfortably aboard—and five or six less comfortably—but the socializing area was open to the healthful breezes.

The V-bottom hull was driven by a six-cylinder 65-horsepower Kermath, so it was not a speedster, although craft of that design took part in cruiser races. The boat had a typical Hacker touch, a forward cockpit, though it bore the Hacker & Fermann label.

As another example, in 1926 an established company in a related field decided to enter boatbuilding. It was the Sterney Woodcraft Company of East Hartford, Connecticut, and it offered a stock 31-footer of Hacker's design. The boat could travel at 15 miles per hour, driven by its four-cylinder, 70-horsepower Scripps engine.

Keel, stem, and frames were of oak. The planking was cedar painted white, the trim was mahogany, and the cabin interior was also finished in mahogany. Copper fastening was used throughout, the plank fastenings being copper rivets over burrs. "The galley is entirely sheathed with burnished copper, and a copper hood is fitted over the stove."

The forward two-thirds of this craft had a raised deck. There was a small bow cockpit as well as the main open deck at the stern, over which was a standing roof that rested on vertical supports—the

standard arrangement for a small cruiser. The control station was at the front of this space. Accommodations consisted of a head in the bow, two sofa berths in the main cabin, and above them two pipe berths. There was enough room in the aft cockpit for two cots. Six people sleeping aboard would have tight comfort. The bow cockpit was unusual in a cruiser of this type, but not in a Hacker design. Otherwise what mainly distinguished the craft was the quality of its construction.

One model exemplifies Hacker cruisers of the mid-1920s. In *Motor Boating* for July 1926 Hacker and Fermann advertised standard 55-foot cruisers, though these boats were semicustom products with many features varied according to the customer's desires. Round-bottom boats, they had oak frames and mahogany planking. Normally they were equipped with two Kermath 100-horsepower engines driving two screws, which produced a maximum speed of 15 miles per hour. A surviving boat, now being restored by Ronald Lane, also had a generator for electricity, a Kelvinator refrigerator, and a pressurized system that provided hot and cold running water. A few of the original features, such as open knife switches for the electrical system, have had to be updated.

The boats had two staterooms and a head under a trunk cabin aft, a large enclosed deck house, and galley, crew's quarters, and head under the raised deck forward. The crew had a more comfortable space on this boat than on many, and its quarters could well be used as another stateroom. There were controls both in the deckhouse and on a raised bridge, the opening of which could be closed with the equivalent of a tonneau cover—it had no windshield.

Lane has the original paperwork, which gives some insight to the Hacker-Fermann relationship. Fermann evidently acted as a broker, bringing together a Hacker design, a purchaser, and a builder—in this case the premier yacht builder, Defoe of Bay City, Michigan. Lane has traced two similar boats constructed in 1926 and one in 1928. There may be others.

Throughout his career Hacker also prepared many stock designs that he sold as Hackerform plans, in a completely separate operation. One of his most popular plans at this time was for a 35-foot cruiser that he called *Sea Bird*, but he had stock designs, which he frequently updated, for many different boats. (A redesigned *Sea Bird*, for example, appeared in *The Rudder*, for May 1932.)

Dolphin and Baby Dolphin, 1926

Dolphins were no longer connected with Bear Cats in advertising. In February 1926 Hacker & Fermann advertised the Hackercraft of that year, a 25-foot, 10-inch Dolphin with a small aft cockpit plus a forward double cockpit in which the controls were located, and a 22-foot Baby Dolphin with the controls aft in a double cockpit and a tiny forward cockpit usually closed with a tonneau cover. There was no windshield. At that time the plant was also building 10 racing runabouts, the Tampa Baybies, which had single cockpits with controls aft and tiny almost useless forward cockpits usually closed with tonneau covers, and of course with no windshields. *Motor Boat* for May 25, 1926, gives the length of the Baby Dolphin as "just under 22 feet." It says the length of the Tampa Bayby was "21 feet 6 inches." The initial Baby Dolphins were almost certainly patterned after the baby racers, except that the Dolphins had larger aft cockpits with two athwartships seats and the engines were moved slightly forward. In the still-limited space of Hacker's shop, it probably was necessary in producing two such models to make them as much alike as possible.

Later that year, after the Tampa Baybies were completed and shipped to Tampa, the Baby Dolphin was also offered with a different layout—a larger but still single forward cockpit protected by a windshield and containing the controls, plus a slightly larger single aft cockpit. ("Popular demand dictated the seating arrangement of the Baby Dolphin shown below.") The Baby had a "gracefully curved deck, artistic polished bronze hardware," and "blue Spanish upholstery." The 25-foot Dolphin was powered by a Scripps F-6 Marine engine, F-6 Junior Gold Cup, or G-6 Marine; the 22-footer by a Scripps F-4, F-6, or Special F-6.

According to one advertisement at the New York and Baltimore Boat Shows, the two Dolphins were "acclaimed by thousands as the most beautiful boats in America." Hacker was becoming known for his artistic eye in designing his boats, which were fast-moving works of sculpture. Their graceful sheer line curved downward toward the bow, a feature that came to be copied by most other builders of runabouts and that can still be seen in boats of the present day. Some even copied the hardware that Hacker designed. Hacker's young son, John A., is quoted as saying that you could recognize the source of another company's boat design by looking at the boats of "the guy they stole it from."

The boats were as seaworthy as they were beautiful. An August 1926 advertisement in *Yachting* reprinted a letter from a well-satisfied customer:

"I received my 22-foot Baby Dolphin boat a week ago Saturday at Greenport and ran it across

A Hacker 35-foot stock-plan Seabird cruiser is shown in March 1927. Hacker sold many stock plans of boats for others to build. "Seabird" was his generic name for cruisers of this type. © *Mystic Seaport, Rosenfeld Collection, Mystic, Connecticut*

Gardner's Bay to Three Mile Harbor. The engine ran perfectly all the way over from the minute we started out at Greenport. I went across the Sound on Friday, June 25, to the Yale-Harvard Boat Race at New London. Coming back that evening we ran into a very heavy sea and the boat went through it beautifully. In fact, I would hesitate to have come across in a boat of such size if it had not acted so well in such rough water from the start. A 35-foot raised deck cruiser, which followed us over, took the sea over its bows several times."

Among the features of the larger Dolphin were its angled windshield, "rigidly reinforced at center." The double cockpit forward was advertised as seating seven. Also included were "Elgin instrument panel under glass, indirectly illuminated and flanked by ignition switch and choke" and "swivel type ventilators of special nontarnishing nickel." The engine hatches still were raised. The large but single aft cockpit contained a "wicker settee, removable and reversible, enabling use of aft cockpit for luggage, etc." There were combination lifting rings and cleats, fore and aft. In the aft deck were fillers for each of the two 25-gallon gas tanks. The transom was brass bound and there was a brass half-round fender.

The new sales arrangement between Hacker and Fermann lasted only about a year. Then the two parted, supposedly so that Hacker could devote full time to building runabouts, but circumstances were vague about his withdrawal from yet another company. He could have been disenchanted with the arrangement; from this distance Fermann seems to have traded on Hacker's name but contributed little. Hacker's daughter Marion may have provided the key when she wrote, "No matter how many people he took into partnership, he ended up buying them out."

McCready's name began to appear publicly in connection with the Hacker Boat Company. In early 1926 the Scripps Motor Company published a full-page advertisement that reprinted a letter from the Hacker Boat Company accompanying an order for "our stock of motor requirements for 1926," and signed by S. D. McCready as "Sect'y & Treas." The following year Scripps reprinted another McCready letter—this time signed over the single word "Treasurer"—addressed to Scripps and saying, "You will doubtless be pleased to learn that we have just shipped one of our new 28 footers to Mr. E. T. Strong, President of the Buick Motor Company, Flint," and going on to tell of

the 150-horsepower Scripps G-6 motor that Strong had specified.

Dolphin and Dolphin Deluxe, 1927

An April 1927 advertisement announced, "Among the many distinctive features of Hackercraft are: Indestructo-glass windshield. Elgin instrument panel. Spring upholstery. White metal deck hardware. Water-tight collision bulkhead. Double plank bottoms. Goodrich rubber bearings. Parsons bronze strut and rudders. To insure absolute safety, heavy bronze plate in hull over propeller."

The first page of the Hackercraft catalog of 1927 was headed "Hackercraft are Thoroughbreds"—a motto similar to one used some years later by Century boats. The catalog offered only two models, the Dolphin and the Dolphin Deluxe, both controlled from forward double cockpits and both with V-shaped windshields for the forward cockpit. Of the Dolphin, a 24-foot boat, it said "Through adoption of certain lines developed by Mr. Hacker it has proved in actual test to be more seaworthy than the 26-foot [actually 25-foot 6-inch] former Dolphin, which was considered one of the best of its

size." The boat was powered by a Scripps Model L Junior Gold Cup engine. About the 28-foot Dolphin Deluxe, it said that it "has the roomiest cockpit of any stock runabout, is a superior performing boat and the fastest marine-engine powered outfit in the field." In this Hacker distanced it from boats with converted aircraft engines, which he distrusted. Here he installed a Scripps Model G

Both Dolphins had come a long way from the boats of 1920, which lacked windshields, had small forward cockpits, and featured large open spaces behind the engines, where there might be wicker chairs. The changes came partly because the engines had shrunk in size, so they could more easily be placed where the designer wanted them. But changes were in large part the result of clever design. Now the forward cockpits had windshields and were more spacious, with two upholstered bench seats that the catalog said could seat seven. The aft cockpit of each was small and had no windshield; it could hold two, also on an upholstered bench. The Dolphin was guaranteed to go faster than 30 miles per hour, the Deluxe Dolphin faster than 37.

Stock boats are under construction at the shop at Mount Clemens in 1926, after Hacker consolidated his building program there. *Courtesy S. Steven McCready*

The 25-foot, 10-inch Hacker Dolphin of 1926 followed what was becoming the standard layout, with controls in a forward double cockpit, engines under hatches amidships, and a small cockpit at the stern. *Classic Boating*

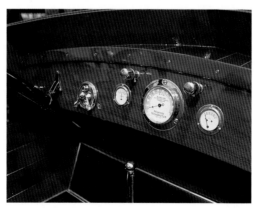

Instrument panel of the 1926 Dolphin. *Classic Boating*

The planking of the boats was of selected mahogany. It was single on the sides with batten-seam construction, double on the bottom with a layer of canvas between the wooden layers. Keel, frames, stem, and battens were of white oak; engine stringers were of spruce; decking, coaming, hatches, and transom were of African mahogany. Covering boards and center plank were "walnutized"—

stained walnut for contrast. All were brass screw fastened and wood plugged. The inside of the hull had two coats of paint, the bottom three coats of green copper paint, and the outside four coats of Valspar varnish.

John L. Hacker's unstoppable drive to produce boats did not improve his family's life, something to which he seemed quite oblivious. His daughter Marion wrote that Hacker was "a conundrum, a simple family man, quite bereft of social graces and grammar, a genius, forever packing to go on trips and face new prospects: the most disruptive events in our family life. Things were always more peaceful when he was away!" He was off to confer with a client about a new design, to supervise the building of one of his boats, or to watch a race in which a boat of his design was competing. Before a race he often would join the crew that was preparing the boat; as a builder himself he was very much a hands-on designer. But then, "when he came home there were exciting tales, and fascinating toys."

Dolphin, Dolphin Jr., and Baby Dolphin, 1928

In 1928 the Hacker Company built an addition to its factory, a new building of reinforced concrete block. By comparison with Chris-Craft, and even with Gar Wood, the Hacker shop had been small and outdated. Hacker probably looked at the others' factories and felt that he needed to expand in order to continue in business, and the McCreadys must have agreed when they financed the added building. By August, the expanded factory had produced between 125 and 130 boats, according to the Mount Clemens *Daily Leader* of August 18.

Now that the new factory permitted increased production, for the first time Hacker offered more than two models and also adjusted the names: "John L. Hacker, dean of American speed-boat designers, has produced his greatest masterpiece in the new 29-foot Dolphin, furnished in both runabout and sedan models." The company now offered two other stock runabouts, a 26-foot Dolphin Jr. and a 24-foot Baby Dolphin. The 29-footer, an 11-passenger craft, had a double cockpit forward, with usual arrangement of an engine compartment under flush hatches, followed by the after cockpit. This model was also available as a sedan, with an enclosed top—much like that of an auto of the day—around the forward double cockpit. Because the enclosed boat needed a pass-through space, the sedan model carried one less person.

Dolphin Jr. could carry nine, as could Baby Dolphin. (None of the advertisements added the words "in comfort" to the maximum number that could be carried.) Standard engines were the Sterling Petrel for Dolphin Deluxe, Scripps H-6 for Dolphin Jr., and Scripps F-6 Gold Cup for Baby Dolphin. The largest boat was able to travel at over 40 miles per hour, as could the middle one; the smallest was rated at 33 miles per hour. All had controls in front cockpits.

This year's 26-footer introduced what became a staple length that lasted through most of the Hacker Boat Company's lifetime. It was apparently the most popular size over the years, and today more 26-footers seem to have been kept and restored than any other model.

The three boats were built of Honduras mahogany, with double bottoms, most of which now were Port Orford cedar. Cedar was lighter in weight and less apt to rot than mahogany, though restorers have found that it did not stand up as well under the pounding of high-powered engines. The stems, keels, and chines were oak, and framing was entirely of oak. The engine bed timbers were

Six-cylinder Scripps engine of the 1926 Dolphin. *Classic Boating*

of spruce and extended the length of the boat. Upholstery was leather, and the sides of the cockpits were lined in leather. The boats had three-piece windshields of shatterproof glass; the center section of each windshield would tilt open for ventilation.

Another May advertisement that year was headlined, "Hackercraft—Always a Year or Two Ahead," and went on to say, "Styles change in boats, just as they do in motor cars or in dress. Many features now in general use were originally introduced by John Hacker in past years." One usually is skeptical of advertising claims, but this one was true. It was generally accepted that Hacker's runabouts were the leaders, and that other manufacturers looked to them for aspects to copy. In addition to their obvious beauty above water, his craft had bottom designs that probably interested the competitors even more.

The ad went on to list some of the current features—largely the result of bottom design—that were less obvious than beautiful appearance, but even more important: "Thrilling speed, free from pounding, free from flying spray, without engine noise or vibration. It skims over the surface of the water, planes always at a low angle, banks inboard on the sharpest turns, and when getting up to speed or slowing down, the whole boat rises or settles bodily without lifting at the bow or squatting at the stern."

Four Dolphins, 1929–1930

At the 1929 New York Boat Show, Hackercraft had more boats to show as a result of its

For 1927 Hacker changed the line, though still producing only two models. The 24-footer was powered by a Scripps Model F Junior Gold Cup engine, which provided a guaranteed speed of over 30 miles per hour. *Courtesy Tom Flood*

On a November day in 1928, John Hacker tries out what was probably the first of his 1929 30-foot "Dolphin Custom Sport Speedsters," which is mildly streamlined. The boat here is so new it has not yet had its running lights fitted. It was offered with either a Kermath or Sterling six-cylinder 225-horsepower engine. © *Mystic Seaport, Rosenfeld Collection, Mystic, Connecticut*

expansion. There was a new 30-foot Dolphin Custom Sport Speedster and the 29-foot Dolphin Deluxe Sedan, each with a 200-horsepower Sterling engine, providing speeds of 41 and 37 miles per hour, respectively. The 26-foot Dolphin, equipped with a 200-horsepower Kermath, would travel at 42 miles per hour in the open model and 40 miles per hour in the sedan. The 24-foot Dolphin, also available in sedan and open models, had a Gray Special Straight Eight, providing 33 and 35 miles per hour. The advance notice in *Yachting* that February added, "John L. Hacker, H. P. Hellmuth [who had become company secretary], and S .D. McCready will be in attendance."

The notice went on to state, "Again for 1929, Hackercraft will set new and higher standards of excellence in runabout design and construction, supplemented by surpassing beauty of line and finish. The creative art of John L. Hacker, internationally accepted as the world's foremost designer of fast pleasure boats, has attained new heights."

It is notable that although Hacker produced ultrastreamlined designs in some of his custom boats—the super runabout *Lockpat II* for instance, or the Gold-Cup racer *Ethyl-Ruth IV*—his stock runabouts were more restrained and never had barrel backs or barrel bows or other extremes of streamlining.

Overseas Recognition

During this time Hacker's son, who was in effect his office manager, collected the stamps from letters that his father received from all over the world. There were more than 100 different ones ranging from all of the European countries to places such as the Ukraine, Colombia, Rhodesia, Straits Settlements, South Africa, and Australia. Hacker was one of the few American designers who were as well known abroad as at home. On one occasion the post office delivered a letter addressed simply to John L. Hacker, N.A—U.S.A.

In 1929 Richard M. Busse, of Berlin, with his 26-foot Hackercraft driven by a 200-horsepower Kermath engine, swept the runabout races in Germany, France, and Italy. In 1930 he reported that in the Berlin-Potsdam regatta, the first of the year, he won the runabout race and the Gabarty Gold Cup for all-around excellence of his boat. In 1931 he won the same cup again with the same boat, as well as several other prizes.

In 1930 Count Anselmi, of Italy, won the Venice-Trieste Race in a Hackercraft, coming in well ahead of the other contestants in rough weather. "I am most satisfied with the results obtained by my Hackercraft, because same is not only quick but also very fit to be used when the sea is rough."

A 1930 report from Port Said, Egypt, said:

"On Sunday morning a small motor boat arrived in harbor, and on reaching the Canal Company's wharf, it was found to be that belonging to Ali Bey Yehia, the son of Ali Bey Pasha. He had come by sea from Alexandria, a distance of 146 nautical miles in 4 1/2 hours. This remarkable feat was accomplished by an American engine, and speaks well, not only for the boat, but for the driving and piloting as well. About 10:15 Ali Bey Yehia and a few friends left Port Said via the Suez Canal for Ismailia, to go thence by fresh water canal for Cairo, and no doubt to complete the round trip to Alexandria by the Nile. The journey from Port Said to Ismailia was made in about 1 hour and 50 minutes."

The boat was a 26-foot Hackercraft powered by a 200-horsepower Kermath. Ali Bey was quoted as saying that the first half of the trip, in open water, was very rough, but that the engine ran smoothly and "we did not get a single drop of water on deck, and the flying spray merely touched the stern, where the seats were naturally covered."

Maximum Production

In the boom years, the Hacker plant worked two shifts. On the verge of the economic precipice, in 1929, it added a "steel building" to its factory. A news clipping headlined, "Good year is forecast for Hacker boats. McCready sees export trade gain and continued domestic demand. Employment increase within few weeks. Enlarged shop provides better facilities for additional production." And that same year the Hacker Boat Company, seeing a growing market, opened a San Francisco branch. "Henry P. Hellmuth, sales manager of the Hacker Boat Co., announces the appointment of S. Clyde Kyle, as San Francisco representative," said *Motor Boat.* Added *Motor Boating,* "A complete display of the Hacker Dolphin runabouts has been arranged in the Rialto Building."

In April 1929, *Motor Boat* published a full-page article headed "The Hacker Phenomenon". After a sketch of Hacker's early history it said, "For the past 20 years he has specialized particularly in fast runabouts and racing boats, bringing out feature after feature, record after record until his boats are now seen on every waterway in the country and his name is known among sportsmen the world over." In describing his boats it commented, "Master design produces a boat that never plunges, never buries on a turn, that lifts bodily when you get under way rapidly and settles when you shut it off."

In May 1929 *Motor Boating* ran an article titled "How Fine Runabouts Are Built," with the subhead, "Plant of the Hacker Boat Company Working at Full Speed on Production of Fine High Speed Runabouts." The plant was well organized, the workers men of skill and pride. "Nowhere in this country, perhaps, will one find closer adherence to the standards of fine workmanship carried to such extremes." Though the plant used machine tools and advanced construction methods, handwork still was at a premium.

"In a short, rather interrupted interview with John Hacker, the point which he constantly stressed was the fact that wood, unlike most materials particularly adapted to production work, responds most favorably to those who understand and react to grain and texture—who, in short, love wood for its beauty, pliancy, and strength." A reader can almost smell the wood shavings. As each boat left the factory, it reminded the reporter of "a perfectly groomed thoroughbred being led to the starting line."

A similar article appeared in *Motor Boat.* Speaking of Hacker, it said, "His creative ability, coupled with the craftsmanship of these experts, has resulted in a number of outstanding models that have seemed to help raise existing standards to a still higher plane." It quoted Hacker: "Wherever machinery can replace handwork it has been done, but we are jealous of our standards. . . too much 'production' is a drawback that is revealed when the boat has been in use a season or two."

During this time, if a customer came to inspect his new stock boat, Hacker would look him over and then often say that because of his weight or height or other characteristic, the seat of his boat should be moved or perhaps some other change should be made. The boat would then go back into the shop for the work, disrupting schedules and adding costs to a craft that would be sold at a stock-boat price. It was more important to Hacker that the boat be right for the buyer than that the company lose money. As a result, the business-oriented office staff did their best to keep any such visitors from meeting the head of the company.

Skilled workers were the backbone of the plant. John Tesmer, the superintendent, in addition to handling general supervision lofted out new boats and made the patterns. Abraham DeHate was in charge of the mill room, where slabs of the

At the Miami Regatta in 1929, the 26-foot Hackercraft *Adriatic,* with a 200-horsepower Kermath engine, won in the runabout class in what was described as "one of the prettiest races of the regatta." Her hatch covers are propped slightly open during the race, probably so that more air can reach the engine, both for cooling and carburetion. ©*Mystic Seaport, Rosenfeld Collection, Mystic, Connecticut*

appropriate wood were turned into wooden boat parts. Another key worker was Al Schlinder, a skilled carpenter who had left Germany in 1907. It was rumored that he had played the violin in a New York orchestra before coming to Detroit. He stayed with the company until it closed.

In April 1929, a full-page advertisement headed "America's Fastest" pictured the *Adriatic,* a 26-foot stock Dolphin with the standard Kermath engine. Racing against other fast stock boats at Palm Beach, it swept the field—nearly lapping it—with an average speed of 41.38 miles per hour. "Hacker design and Hacker workmanship present a significant combination of beauty, speed and staunchness to the distinguished roll of Hackercraft owners." A September advertisement listed 18 places in the United States where the boats could be seen, plus "London, England, 23 Orchard Street, W.I., Mayfair." Hacker did not follow the extreme automobile sales methods of Chris-Craft, but it did let people know where its products could be found.

Hackercraft's Competitive Pricing

Because Hackercraft were known as the Steinways of runabouts, one is apt to think of them as expensive. They were not cheap, but a comparison with other makes is surprising. The June 1930 issue of *Motor Boat* printed a table comparing the prices of runabouts produced by several builders. (The prices also give some idea of inflation since then.) Hacker prices occupied a middle ground from $3,100 to $5,700. Dodge started at under $1,000 and ended at about $5,000. Chris-Craft went from $1,200 to $7,000. Lyon ranged from $2,600 to $6,500. The biggest spread and the highest top price applied to Gar Wood's boats, which went from $2,200 to $12,950.

These were prices for runabouts only. Cruisers were not included, although some of the more expensive Gar Wood boats appear to have been such borderline cases as limousines and commuters. The Hacker prices shown did not include commuters or custom-designed boats.

In its boat show edition in February 1930, *Yachting* took special notice of the Hacker 24-footer. "It is a very fast, staunch model that handles with surprising ease and quickness, and in which are incorporated the singularly beautiful lines that characterize the speed boat designs of John L. Hacker."

The company was careful to give news of some of its sales to *Yachting,* which of all the boating magazines had the most upscale readers. In September 1930, Hacker announced that it now had a 30-foot duo-sedan, driven by the standard 225-horsepower Kermath. There was an open driver's seat in front of a small sedan top built over the rear seat in the forward cockpit. The effect was much like that of an automobile town-car of the time, with an open driver's seat ahead of an enclosed passenger cabin. This boat, it said, had gone to Mrs. John T. Fitzgerald, of Chicago, for use on Rainy Lake in Minnesota.

In December there was a photo of a 40-mile-an-hour 30-foot runabout built by Hacker for "C.P. McCready of Akron, Ohio." The boat was flying along with cockpits full of passengers. No mention was made that this was the man who had underwritten the expanded Hacker factory.

Runabout Races, 1930

Hacker's stock boats continued to distinguish themselves in runabout races, providing positive advertisement for his products. In December 1930 *Motor Boating* reported:

"Glancing over the records of the regattas held during the past motor boating season, one is impressed with the remarkable series of winnings which have fallen to the lot of the popular Hackercraft.

"One of the most outstanding of the successful performers was John Rutherfords' Hackercraft *Becky,* powered with a 225-horsepower Kermath. At Annapolis he won a first and a second in two different events, and at Bellport, Long Island, he took another first place. Other winnings included second in one of the Gold Cup Regatta events, a first and second in two events in the President's Cup Regatta and two firsts at New Bedford.

"Other Hackercraft placed first or second in many events throughout the country—at Palm Beach, Bay Shore, Long Island, Severn River, Herald Harbor, the Pass Christian, Regattas on the Gulf of Mexico, Lake George, Lake Champlain, Detroit, Portland, Maine and many other prominent regattas throughout the country. Other victories included first and second prizes at Potsdam, Germany; Trieste, Italy; and Canada."

The Hacker Boat Company was flourishing. One estimate has placed the high point for Hacker production at June 1930, and says that the company employed about 150 people then and that they delivered 90 boats that month. In 1930 Hacker and his family moved from Detroit to a new home in the suburb of St. Clair Shores that was described as his dream house. This removed them from the close proximity of other members of the large Hacker family, but they still participated in the constant round of family gatherings: card games, dinners, birthdays, graduations, confir-mations, weddings, funerals—any excuse for a party. This seems to have been about the only socializing that John Hacker enjoyed.

Hacker must have felt a twinge when that same year his old colleague, Joe Van Blerck, was somehow maneuvered out of the engine company he had founded, though it continued to use his name. But there was little that Hacker could do; the Hacker Boat Company did not make engines.

The Century Boats Connection

Under the major heading "Outboard Notes" and a secondary heading of "Century Boat Reorganized," the April 1930 issue of *Motor Boating* published an announcement:

"The Century Boat Company of Manistee, Michigan, has undergone a reorganization, which puts them in a position to handle better the production of the outboard boats. The business was purchased in November of 1929 by George G. Eddy, who organized a new closed corporation to carry out an extensive manufacturing and development campaign. John A. Hacker, son of the well-known designer, John L. Hacker, of Detroit and Mt. Clemens, was elected president, Ard E. Richardson, of Lansing, vice-president and treasurer, and George G. Eddy, of Manistee, secretary and general manager."

The first four workmen were hired on November 13, and John L. Hacker was commissioned to turn his genius toward the creation of the new boats.

This happened not long after the younger Hacker graduated from the City College of Detroit (today's Wayne State University). It seemed to be a good opportunity for him to establish himself. The article listed a mixture of outboard and light inboard boats that the company would produce. In addition to several outboard boats there was:

"The new Mermaid model, [which] is undoubtedly destined to achieve the greatest popularity of all, being a 17-foot six-passenger

runabout that combines outboard portability and inboard stability. A compact stern installation, entirely inboard, of Caille's new development in 22-horsepower powerheads driving through the new patented Hacker drive unit, with a Caille reversing propeller, makes possible wonderful performance qualities and full maneuverability in a 25-mile runabout."

In addition there was a 19-foot Aristocrat model with a Universal engine, also driving through the Hacker unit.

Contents of the 1930 Century catalog were slightly different. It listed three boats that it credited to John L. Hacker. Two were outboard boats: the 17-foot Traveler, an earlier model that he dressed up so that it looked like a small runabout, and the 12-foot, 8-inch outboard racer called the Cyclone. In addition there was the 17-foot inboard Seamaid, using the Caille powerhead and Hacker drive.

But then the January 1931 *Motor Boating* published an article by George Eddy, general manager of Century, which told that the Century plant was being enlarged as a result of increased sales. Peculiarly, no mention was made of John L. Hacker's designs, and the president of the company, who was pictured, was now A. E. Richardson, not John A. Hacker. Where had all the Hackers gone?

There was a complete and sudden break between Century and the Hackers. The following February 31 issue of *Motor Boat*, under the heading, "Century Announces Inboard Runabouts," listed four Sea Maids, the largest a five-passenger, 38 mile-per-hour boat, "with the chummy forward cockpit." Only the 17-foot Century Sea Maid (which now had a Universal Blue Jacket engine) was credited to John L. Hacker in the caption for its picture, and nothing was said about Mermaids, Aristocrats, or Cyclones. The company had changed direction and was now emphasizing inboard rather than outboard models. There was a small inboard racing boat, the Thunderbolt, which could be used to race in the 151 class or the International 2-liter class. (Hacker was not credited with designing the Thunderbolt, as has sometimes been suggested. Century historians do not believe that it was his design or that he ever designed any further boats for Century.)

The sudden disappearance of the Hackers was in a sense lucky for them. The purchasers of the Century company had unwittingly chosen the worst possible time, on the brink of the depression, to start what was essentially a new business. On September 2, 1932, Century declared bankruptcy. A. E. Richardson, one of the original group and recently the president, bought the Century company and installed his own officers—the

The Hacker home in Saint Clair Shores, Michigan, a Detroit suburb. The house was completed for them in 1930 and the Hacker family moved in. *Courtesy Marion Hacker Hurst*

Hackers were not among them—under whom it limped ahead, gradually improving its position as the depression eased.

The Hackers' brief dance with Century probably came to an end because of the change in Century's policy, shifting its production from light powered craft to runabouts that, at least in a general way, competed with Hackercraft. That most likely caused the Hackers to withdraw. If they did not leave of their own volition, S. Dudley McCready would have called John L. back. Designing runabouts for Century would be clearly in violation of his contract with the McCreadys.

The elder Hacker was never president of Century, as has sometimes been suggested. Although he designed a few of its light early boats, no evidence has been found that he designed any others for Century.

The Muskoka Lakes Connection

Hacker had a longstanding connection with the boatbuilders on the Muskoka Lakes, in Canada. It may have begun when one of them, Bert Minett, worked for him over a couple of years early in the century. It may also have been sparked by Harry Greening, a Canadian powerboat enthusiast who lived in Hamilton, Ontario, but had most of his boats built on the Muskokas. Greening commissioned a cruiser from Hacker before 1920.

Minett was born and grew up on a farm on the shores of Lake Rosseau, one of the Muskokas.

He returned home and set up as a boatbuilder in the town of Bracebridge on Lake Muskoka.

In the mid-1920s Hacker designed a 24-foot and a 26-foot boat for Minett. The Muskoka builders did not have the extensive market available to American builders; Minett apparently produced two of each. Probably a few of his succeeding boats were loosely based on the Hacker designs.

Bert Minett, like Hacker, was a perfectionist, and like Hacker he had very little business sense. He was about to go bankrupt in 1925 when a young summer resident named Bryson Shields bought into the company, which became Minett-Shields. In 1929 Minett-Shields built a 38-foot, two-step launch designed by Hacker. Built for a Muskoka summer resident, J. Y. Murdoch, *Wimur II* is usually considered the ultimate Minett-Shields boat, coming as it did on the threshold of the depression. In 1934 Hacker designed an 18-foot "sports runabout" as a stock model for a much less affluent Minett-Shields. He also on occasion designed a few boats for other Muskoka builders.

Without being able to read Hacker's agreement with the McCreadys, it is hard to say why his work for outside builders in the Muskokas did not bring objections. Perhaps the Hacker Boat Company received a percentage of his fees. Perhaps the boats were built outside the country and thus outside the agreement.

Tom Greavette broke away from the old Muskoka company of Ditchburn, where he was a director, and set up his own business in 1929. He was backed by a group of affluent men and became a major figure in the area.

About 1933 Hacker agreed to design all of Greavette's boats in an arrangement that lasted until 1937. For part of that time Greavette was also the sole Canadian boatbuilder for whom he did designs, though the beginnings of that arrangement are uncertain; after all, there was the Minett-Shields sports runabout of 1934.

In either 1935 or 1936 (accounts vary) Greavette launched the *Curlew*, a torpedo-shaped 33-footer designed by Hacker. A beautiful boat, it was reminiscent of Hacker's somewhat longer *Lockpat II*, a custom design of 1931 for Detroit sportsman Dick Locke. To help Greavette's people learn how to build the rounded hull, Hacker took with him on one of his trips to Greavette a skilled boatbuilder, probably John Tesmer. Greavette built not only *Curlew*, but also a transom-sterned near duplicate. Smaller transom-sterned boats suggested by this design—so-called "streamliners"—followed.

A 26-foot Hutchinson boat of 1930 originally named *Kit* shows one way that Hacker's influence spread. Workmen for Hutchinson, on the upper St. Lawrence River, crossed the ice in the winter to a boathouse where a 1929 Hackercraft was stored and took off the lines. Five or six boats were made from them, some shortened, some the original 30 feet long. The dark stain on the mahogany was originally made from black paint thinned with turpentine. The original engine is not known, but a 290-horsepower Chrysler Hemi now powers it. *Classic Boating*

Five Dolphins, 1931

A Hackercraft catalog issued about 1931 reflects the height of Hacker prosperity—somewhat after the fact, although no one knew that when it was published. At the bottom of each page was printed a line taken from some letter complimenting the boats. The letters originated all over the United States, and in Canada, Mexico, Germany, Sweden, Italy, England, Holland, and Egypt.

An early page of the catalog said, "Nothing plays so important a part in the creation of the boat as design, and in the entire industry, unchallenged leadership is freely conceded to John Hacker, Naval Architect, who has for 36 years been eminent in the creation of fine, fast speed boats and cruisers."

The smallest boat offered for sale was a 22 1/2-foot Hackercraft, which was, the catalog suggested, the ideal choice for smaller lakes, rivers, and protected waters. Another page described this same boat as the ideal tender for the most luxurious yacht. But the bulk of the publication was taken up by larger boats: 24-, 26-, 28-, and 30-footers.

The 22 1/2-footer had a Chrysler Royal 82-horsepower engine or Kermath 6 with 80 horsepower. The 24-footer had either a Gray 140-horsepower straight eight or a Chrysler Six Imperial of 125 horsepower. The 26-, 28-, and 30-footers all had six-cylinder Kermaths with 225 horsepower. Today the 30-footer is probably the most sought-after boat for restoration.

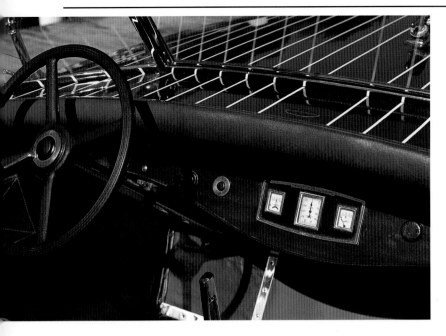

The driver's station of *Kit. Classic Boating*

the sides screw fastened. The 30-, 35-, and 38-footers had both their sides and their bottoms copper and bronze riveted.

About 1929 Hacker completed a series of experiments on hull design. When traveling head-on into steep waves at some speed, the bow of a boat with a concave V-bottom could slam down so hard that at times the impact would threaten the structure of the boat, to say nothing of the comfort of its passengers. He developed a bottom that retained the basic V-shape but that was slightly convex, rounding outward rather than inward. This shape cushioned the impact when, after riding a steep wave, the bow moved suddenly downward and hit the water. He devised a speed-power formula that indicated when such a bottom would be desirable. Many of his smaller boats still retained the concave V-bottom, but he began to design his larger, faster ones with convex bottoms.

As Hacker Company produced its greatest number of boats during these prosperous times, and that the company's future boats, at least until World War II, appear to have followed the same specifications, the construction details are of some interest.

The 22 1/2-footer and the 24-footer each had 48 frames—12 main, 6 intermediate, 30 small. The 26-footer had 54—14 main, 8 intermediate, 32 small. The 28-footer, oddly, had 53—15 main,

Construction

Getting down to more basic facts, two full pages described hull construction for all the boats. "Construction: White Oak, Spruce, and Mahogany." Honduras mahogany planking was used throughout. Bottoms were double planked with it. In the 22 1/2-footer and the 24-footer, the bottoms were screw fastened. The 26- and 28-footers' bottoms were bronze and copper riveted,

In 1931 the 30-foot Hackercraft *Musketeer II,* with a 200-horsepower Sterling engine, won the runabout race at Miami— with eight boats contending—under new American Powerboat rules. © *Mystic Seaport, Rosenfeld Collection, Mystic, Connecticut*

A 32-foot Hackercraft runabout introduced in late 1931, as the Great Depression deepened, was the ultimate Hackercraft design. The depression, followed by World War II, largely ended the era of big runabouts of this classic pattern, though Hackercraft was the one builder that for many years would continue offering standard runabouts. © *Mystic Seaport, Rosenfeld Collection, Mystic, Connecticut*

6 intermediate, 32 small. The 30-footer had 59— 13 main, 12 intermediate, 34 small. Essentially the frames were lighter than, for example, those in Chris-Craft, but more numerous. All keels were white oak.

The catalog did not explain a curiosity that restorers of these boats have found. In a boat with double bottom planking, the inner layer is laid diagonally, the angled planks on each side meeting at the keel line. The two angled sides coming together form something like an arrowhead pattern. In most other boats—Gar Woods and Chris-Crafts—the arrow points toward the stern.

In Hacker boats it points toward the bow. No doubt Hacker had some good reason for this peculiarity, but no one has discovered it.

The publication told that the decking was also Honduras mahogany, although the covering boards and center plank were "mahoganized"— stained a contrasting mahogany color. All were screw fastened and wood plugged. Seams were filled with white composition. Inside, the seat fronts were mahogany, the seat backs plywood— the only place where that material was mentioned.

On all boats, all bright work was given five to seven coats of Valspar varnish. "No higher finish is used in grand pianos." The standard list of accessories went on for an entire paragraph, but for the smaller boats, amenities such as "hatch lock and cigar lighter" were $15 extra.

A full page devoted to the Hacker shops was headed "Hackercraft are built in a modern plant under the direct supervision of John L. Hacker, N.A." Photos showed the overhead track that could move hulls around the plant, the mill room where mahogany arrived in slabs and was turned into boat parts, a long production line, and finally a boat hanging from a lift that was about to put it on the water.

Maintenance

At about the same time, the company issued a booklet called "Lubrication—Care and Operation of the Hackercraft." Reading it, one is reminded that in those days interstate highways and trucks capable of highway speeds did not exist; the boats were shipped by rail. The first instructions in what amounts to an owner's manual tell how to unfasten the boat from the floor of "the car" and unload it. Launching is explained. Instructions follow on putting the flag poles in their proper locations (and connecting the light at the tip of the aft flagpole), connecting the battery, filling the gas tanks and running the electric pumps briefly to bring gas to the carburetor, and putting the mooring lines in place. So far the book continues the excitement of new ownership, the feeling that one is setting out on an adventure. But what follows describes the considerable lubrication and frequent maintenance required, including care of the craft's bottom— scrubbing off the barnacles that could accumulate in salt water and using antifouling paint. A would-be owner who reads the back section first might change his or her mind about buying a boat.

35- and 38-Foot Hackercraft Commuters, 1930–1931

In 1930 Hacker delivered the custom 38-foot express cruiser for the king of Siam. Its production seems to have been linked with that of the 38-foot cruiser-commuter that was offered that year as a stock boat, satisfying a general market developing for such craft. Commuters— fast boats that carried their owners between home and office—seem first to have developed in and around New York City. High-powered yachts carried wealthy men, who mainly had homes on Long Island, to and from the metropolis. But commuting boats, at first in more modest form,

also linked the summer homes of rich Detroiters, which were usually on the shores of Lake St. Clair, with their workplaces. Hacker's 1906 boats for the lumber barons were early examples.

The Hacker Company was well aware of this market. As early as 1928, the Mount Clemens *Daily Leader* of September 29 reported:

"Inquiries on hand for between 20 and 23 new type hydroplanes for use by New York commuters living along Long Island Sound will result in the beginning of production during the next 60 days of a new 34-foot hydroplane by the Hacker Boat Works, it was announced yesterday afternoon."

The 60 days extended to a year and a half, and the first commuters produced were 38-footers, probably because development of the special boat for the king of Siam intervened.

As the interest in commuters grew, Hacker was much involved. C. Philip Moore's "Commuter Register" in his book *Yachts in a Hurry* lists a dozen of Hacker's custom boats that were built during the 1920s and 1930s. Some were for buyers in Detroit, but others went to New York, New Jersey, Massachusetts, Illinois, and Ontario. The name "commuter" soon was attached to almost any fast day boat or cruiser. In the affluent 1920s many buyers, whether they commuted or not, wanted a commuter just to be in fashion.

Other builders responded. To meet this interest, Chris-Craft in 1929 brought out its 38-foot "Commuting Cruiser." Driven by a Chris-Craft 250-horsepower V-8, with varnished topsides and a raised open bridge, it was highly attractive. Through 1931, Chris-Craft sold 65 of the boats. Probably not many actually were used as commuters in the strict sense, but they enabled people to feel that they were speeding along fully in vogue.

Hacker had designed express cruisers with controls on a raised open bridge, but he made his stock boats for his company pure Hackercraft. They had an open driver's cockpit in front, followed by an enclosed sedanlike cabin with windows, and just aft of the cabin windows were enclosed areas—except for small port holes on port and starboard—where head and galley were situated on opposite sides of the boat. Engines were boxed-in under flush hatches behind the cabin, one engine on each side, with a passage between them to a stern cockpit.

The stock boat was powered by two Kermaths, each of 225 horsepower, which drove through twin screws, giving the boat a speed of 42 miles per hour, somewhat less than the king's boat, which could do 63 miles per hour. On other pages, the 1931

catalog had basic information about construction and equipment, but the page that first showed this boat was headed "Now! A Twin Screw 42 Mile-an-Hour Commuter Cruiser," and spoke of it being "the ideal fast commuter," done with "the touch of master design," and "by that artist in naval architecture, John L. Hacker."

A smaller commuter—actually a 35-footer rather than the 34-footer proposed in the 1928 news report—had the same cabin and cockpit layout as the larger craft. It first appeared nearly a year after the larger boat. It was driven by twin Gray 140-horsepower engines that could move the boat at 30 to 33 miles per hour. It was basically an adaptation for family cruising as well as for commuting. From the family viewpoint, said the catalog, it "provides relaxation, joyous adventure, and interesting exploration over a week-end that would require a whole week's absence from the office in the slower type boat."

Construction of these two boats was explained in the 1931 catalog. Materials and finish were the same as for the larger runabouts. For the 35-foot commuter, the main frames were spaced 26 inches apart, the intermediate bent frames were spaced 13 inches apart. On the 38-footer, the main frames were spaced at 28 inches, the intermediate bent frames at 14 inches. Again the frames were relatively light but numerous.

Hacker boats were used by companies and government bodies. In 1931, after the dams were built that produced the 129-mile-long Lake of the Ozarks, the Union Electric Land and Development Company bought a 38-foot commuter and a 24-foot runabout for inspection work. That same year the U.S. Corps of Engineers bought a 24-foot sedan that was shipped to New Orleans to be an inspection boat for flood relief activities on the Lower Mississippi. At Mackinac Island, the firm of Pfeiffelman & Son was one of many throughout the country that operated water taxis, in this case a Hacker and a Chris-Craft. The Hackercraft was a Scripps-powered 26-footer, bought used in 1926. After two years, the engine was replaced with a new Scripps. The boat "has made numerous trips of 6 to 12 miles when cruisers have been laying to for weather. On two occasions the boat was pounded so hard as to break the bottoms out of the front seat [evidently the boat did not have the newer convex bottom], but as yet a rib or frame was never broken, and last but not least, the boat does not leak a drop."

The 32-Foot Runabout, 1931–1932

In addition to its other boats, Hackercraft in late 1931 brought out what was in many ways its ultimate runabout, a 32-footer with a 12-cylinder Kermath "Sea Raider" engine—a new design—that drove the boat at a speed of 55 miles per hour. *Yachting* magazine commented on the boat's "extreme luxuriousness." Probably the company was responding to the 33-footers that Gar Wood, its closest competitor, had built for some years.

Later the boat would be stretched to 33 feet. There is no record of how many 32- and 33-footers were actually produced.

The Great Depression

By 1931 the Hacker Boat Company was beginning to feel the pinch of the Great Depression. Hacker production figures have been lost, but those for Gar Wood show that in 1930 Wood sold 193 boats, but in 1931 only 32. The Hacker Company added a few larger models, including the luxurious 32-foot runabout and a redesigned 28-foot sedan. In a splashy full-page advertisement, it offered the 28-foot runabout at $5,000, "completely equipped." (Its catalog price was $4,975.) But generally Hacker moved down market, adding a 20-foot runabout and promoting the next smallest boat, the 22 1/2-foot runabout. One magazine reviewer said, "Noteworthy features of this model are its low price, deep freeboard, and large cockpits."

But the market for runabouts almost vanished during the depression. The Hacker Boat Company faced this downturn burdened with a new, large plant that now produced little. By contrast, at about this time the Lyman factory changed from making outboard motor boats to white-painted lapstrake inboards that it called "utilities," and they carried it through the depression. The cruiser builders Matthews and Richardson actually grew and profited during the depression years.

No doubt the runabout market had been saturated by many builders who turned out the boats in large numbers during the boom years. If you needed a runabout, good used ones were readily available from virtually any boat dealer. The problem was that few people wanted runabouts.

Anyone who had some money during that period might want to put it into tangible things such as boats rather than risk it in banks, which often failed, or in securities, which often became worthless. The histories of Lyman and the cruiser builders support that theory. The glossy, fast runabouts were far more noticeable, and they were expensive to run and maintain. The runabouts seemed to flaunt their owners' well-being at a time when unemployed workers were lining up at the soup kitchens. Runabouts always were conspicuous—that was part of the fun—but this was not a time for conspicuous consumption.

Hackercraft commuters had all the negative impact of runabouts, multiplied. They were in effect bigger and flashier runabouts. They cost much more to operate and keep up; they could

not help being in public view; and their shape, varnish, chrome, and speed made them the height of conspicuous consumption. The few people who actually needed a commuter might still buy one, but the boats were no longer fashionable. A white-painted cruiser, even if it had a good turn of speed, somehow was less offensive.

Other builders faced the same problems. Chris-Craft survived the depression only through the tenacity of the Smith family, luck, and some very clever financial juggling. Gar Wood survived the depression because Gar Wood himself was a millionaire and was willing to support his boatbuilders. Dodge, probably best known after the other three, moved into a fine new factory—and foundered.

John A. Hacker, son of John L., was also a member of the Hacker Boat Company's board, which consisted of the two McCreadys and the two Hackers. In May 1933, that board approved a request by John L. Hacker that instead of "drawing an amount" from each sale of a boat, he be allowed to draw it on the completion of each boat. In other words, instead of being paid a royalty on boats that were sold, he would be paid for the boats that had been built but were standing unsold in the factory. John L. must have been seriously in need of money, but the move could scarcely help the struggling company.

Black Knight, **one of the attractive 18-foot racing runabouts built to Hacker plans by Minett-Shields on the Muskoka Lakes in 1934. It was of a size more in tune with the future.** *Courtesy Muskoka Lakes Museum*

Eagles' Nest, a restored Hacker runabout of uncertain date. Despite Hacker's advocacy of the forward cockpit, in the early 1920s he designed to order many boats of this more conservative form. *Classic Boating*

Chapter Three

Custom Masterpieces
Unique Hacker Creations

Some of John L. Hacker's finest work was seen in the custom designs he produced throughout his career. They show the variety of his talent. He could turn out a plain, simple boat or an elaborate and innovative one. All of those runabouts and cruisers of many sizes and types gave him the opportunity to expand his ideas and develop new features. For any artistic perfectionist, custom work was ideal. As with so much that he did, there are no records to say how many custom boats came from his drawing boards, but they certainly made up a large part of the 1,000 designs he did in his lifetime.

Hacker also designed fast custom runabouts. In 1921, one two-cockpit runabout—32 feet, 6 inches overall—was built for a La Crosse, Wisconsin, man by the Winona Boat and Machine Company. Powered by a six-cylinder Hall-Scott engine, almost a Hacker standard at that time, it was speedy. But as *The Rudder* put it that September, "The new boat is not intended as an extreme high-speed craft, but rather as an all-purpose runabout." The location of the controls had now become a point of general interest: "In this boat the steering wheel is to be located in the after cockpit, although many of the same type have the wheels forward."

A second design, shown in the July issue of *The Rudder*, was a 36-footer with a six-cylinder Hall-Scott; it was said to have a speed of 35 miles per hour. There was an open forward cockpit; in place of the after cockpit was a glassed-in cabin that could seat seven close friends. The wheel was at the front of this structure, so that the helmsman looked forward through the windshield over the deck.

In 1922 *Motor Boating* published a series of Hacker designs, making them available to the boating public and offering blueprints at nominal prices. Although Hacker advertised, quite rightly, that he was a pioneer of the forward-cockpit layout in runabouts, the five runabouts that he included in this series all had aft cockpits. The 16-foot craft had seats only for the driver and one other person, who sat beside him. The 18-, 20-, 22-, and 28-footers had an additional back seat for two or three passengers. But it is puzzling that all were rear-cockpit boats; perhaps the editors of the magazine felt that the aft-cockpit arrangement was still the normal one.

In its December 1925 issue, *Motor Boat* magazine published a Hacker design for a runabout intended for amateur builders. A 23-footer, it could travel at up to 30 miles per hour with an LKB Loew-Knight motor "or equal"—Scripps F-6 or F-4 and Kermath 50 among them. It had flare forward and tumble home aft. But as in his earlier designs for *Motor Boating*, this boat had only an aft cockpit. The space was relatively large, having two cushioned bench seats some distance apart, which left room for "two small chairs." It then could carry a total of seven passengers. The cockpit coaming rose slightly at its front and was angled backward, but there was no glass windshield. Perhaps it was the relatively small size of the boat that led to the cockpit-aft arrangement, but for the man who pioneered forward cockpits and forward controls, it seems peculiar.

Though Hacker in 1930 made commuter cabin boats up to 38 feet long, beginning in the 1920s he designed several custom runabouts that were that length or longer. They often were described as commuters, though lacking cabins or any bad-weather protection, they were eminently unsuitable for commuting on a daily basis. But the elegance of his runabout designs reached their ultimate in these beauties.

A 1923 Hacker design of a 40-footer for an East Coast owner had an enlarged passenger space forward. It had a windshield in front of what was described as a cockpit, though it held two rows of two bucket seats each and a final upholstered bench that could easily seat three. The space for passengers was in effect an open lounge deck. There was a real cockpit at the stern, behind the engine. It had no windshield but could hold two people and was "arranged for the mechanic."

A boat this large needed a paid hand to take care of it. On a cruiser he probably would be given the courtesy title of captain, but here the term mechanic, which seems to have carried over from racing practice, applied to the caretaker who certainly needed to have mechanical skills. In the engine space under the hatches of this handsome craft rode a 30-gallon oil tank, tools, and what was described as a "shelve," but probably was a small work bench. This mechanic was provided with everything necessary to maintain the 400-horsepower engine.

In a 1926 design under the Hacker & Fermann label, Hacker carried his ideas a bit further. This boat was only 38 feet long and was described as a special runabout rather than a commuter. It had a V-transom, composed of two flat sides that met at a sharp angle, essentially making it a double-ender. The tumble home aft accentuated the sharp stern, carrying the deck back to a pointed end.

This construction approached the attractive form later described by that ugly term, "barrel back." The designer explained that it was essentially a 35-footer with an extended stern to support the rudder, which in turn supported the aft end of the propeller shaft—an arrangement copied from some of the Gold Cup boats.

It had two forward cockpits, each with one upholstered bench seat and each with its own windshield. Under the deck in the space between them was an icebox amidships and a clothing locker on either side (presumably for heavy weather gear). The third cockpit—which had no windshield—was a small one far back; no mention was made of a mechanic, but it looked much like the mechanic's hole on the earlier boat. The framing of this runabout was of oak, elm, and spruce, and its planking was of Honduras mahogany, double planked on sides and bottom. Its bottom of course was Hacker's usual

concave V-bottom. With the 650-horsepower Liberty engine, it was a "mile-a-minute boat."

This series of large, impressive runabouts culminated in 1931, when the custom department of the Hacker Boat Company produced *Lockpat II* for former racing driver Dick Locke. This was as the full force of the depression hit the Hacker Company, when stock runabout and commuter sales were minimal, but Locke purchased the craft that he wanted. A beautiful, 40-foot-long, 7-foot beam, mahogany torpedo with chrome accents, the boat was equipped with a 650-horsepower 12-cylinder Packard engine that drove it over 60 miles per hour, and also with a 40-horsepower trolling engine, both of them under the flush hatches amidships. The sides of

this streamlined runabout were rounded and its sloping stern narrowed down to what looked above water like nothing so much as the bow of a smaller boat turned upside down. There were two forward cockpits, the second of which had no windshield and had a flush hatchcover when not in use. Each cockpit was said to hold four people comfortably, although in photos the aft cockpit seems the smallest. Front and rear cockpits had a metal framed, V-shaped windshield. The boat was said to be a commuter that would carry Locke between his home, 40 miles away, and Detroit.

Powerboating for November 1931 wrote, "Construction is barrel type. Framing is white oak and spruce, planking [Honduras mahogany] of double thickness on sides and bottom, inner laid

Dick Locke, owner of *Lockpat II,* has the hatches open to display the second front cockpit and the engine. © *Mystic Seaport, Rosenfeld Collection, Mystic, Connecticut*

diagonally, outer fore and aft. Over 22,000 fastenings are used, and three watertight bulkheads insure maximum safety." *The Rudder* in October of the following year also described the boat and added, "A telephone connects the driver's cockpit with the mechanics at the stern."

Commuting in this creation in fine weather would be lovely, but 40 miles in rainy, or cold, or windy weather, in open cockpits? And a commuter with a trolling engine? In fact *Lockpat II* seems to have been a super runabout, a beautiful work of art that must have delighted its sportsman owner, and must have given Hacker the commission of a lifetime. At the next Harmsworth International Race, it was part of the spectator fleet, and attracted much attention. (The boat still exists, and at this writing is being restored.)

Custom Cruisers and Commuters

Hacker also was becoming well known for his cruisers. A 1921 design, this one with a 42-foot, 6-inch V-bottom hull, for Webb Jay of Chicago, was of a day cruiser with an unusual cabin layout. A slightly larger version of his 1920 boat *Mary K,* this one had a small driver's cabin in the bow, with a back seat that could be converted into a berth, followed by what the plans called a bridge deck— a flat, open deck, railed in for safety, above the twin Hall-Scott engines—followed by a slightly larger cabin containing a head, a tiny galley, and two settee-berths. Essentially it was a large runabout with cabins over forward and aft cockpits; probably it was of slightly heavier build than a runabout, though only slightly—Hacker seldom built a boat with a truly heavy structure. *Motor Boating* described the boat as a "speed day cruiser" in March of that year.

Hacker is remembered for his elaborate cruisers, but he also designed a number of unpretentious boats that did not as easily catch the eyes of nautical journalists. In 1922 *Motor Boating* published a series of his designs of various kinds of boats. Unlike the designs that the magazine published each month as news items, these were complete with the lines, offsets, and specifications. They all were too complex for amateur builders, but they were provided gratis for more experienced workers and blueprints were offered at a nominal price.

In this series were plans for a 31-foot cruiser, a good example of the designer's more modest work, said to be similar to one that he had produced for himself. This boat, a raised deck model, had a nice touch: a forward cockpit, a feature Hacker was said to enjoy in his own boat. (Hacker's daughter

Lockpat II was a complete departure from the usual Hacker hull and showed the designer's ability to design the streamlined boats popular in the 1930s and early 1940s. A 40-foot torpedo-shaped runabout of 1931, it could do over 60 miles per hour with its 650-horsepower Packard engine. A telephone connected the driver to the aft cockpit, where a mechanic usually rode. Her streamlined shape is quite different from other Hacker boats up to this time. © *Mystic Seaport, Rosenfeld Collection, Mystic, Connecticut*

Throughout his career, Hacker designed cruisers. In the early 1920s several of his express cruisers, such as *Hazel S.,* were essentially enlarged runabouts with cabins over forward and aft cockpits. *The Mariners' Museum, Newport News, Virginia*

Most Hacker cruisers followed the normal pattern of their day and did not move at express speeds. A typical Hacker boat of the mid-1920s, *Jeanne II* has the open bridge that was then normal, though cruisers of this size soon developed wheelhouses combined with living rooms. Note the chairs on the bridge for open-air repose. *The Mariners' Museum, Newport News, Virginia*

reports that the family never had its own boat, though from time to time they were taken on other's boats. Maybe, like many people, Hacker had a dream boat that he never built.) His fast cruisers often had forward cockpits, but in more humble boats they were uncommon. Like those in the fancier boats, this one was to have a canvas cover when it was not in use.

As the magazine said, "The interior arrangement is very compact." There was a head in the bow, partly tucked under the forward cockpit, a berth on either side of the main cabin, and another berth on the starboard side with the feet under the main (after) cockpit. There was a tiny galley, complete with icebox. (This necessary item for carrying fresh food was used before practical electric refrigerators could be put in boats, and no doubt raised memories of Hacker's father's coal and ice business.) The sturdy, high-sided, V-bottom hull with considerable flare at the bow to keep that cockpit dry was said to do 10 miles per hour with a 20-horsepower Kermath engine. The speed could be increased by 3 or 4 miles per hour, but *Motor Boating* warned, "it will take fully 50 horsepower to give the additional few miles in speed. The most economical rate for this boat is the one to be secured with the specified motor, which will do about 5 miles to the gallon of gasoline."

Hacker and Fermann

In 1922 Hacker joined William Fermann in what was called the Hacker & Fermann Company. It was to design larger craft—much more elaborate than the *Motor Boating* design—and act as a yacht brokerage. Some of the cruisers designed and built during that combination are credited to Hacker & Fermann, though Hacker was the designer and Fermann the businessman. The firm is said to have popularized the large raised deckhouse, walk-around decks, and dual controls—in the deckhouse and on the bridge—all features that later became standard.

A 1923 Hacker & Fermann cruiser was the 55-foot *Skylark II,* built by Defoe in Bay City, Michigan. Cedar planked and copper fastened, with mahogany deck structures, it was driven by two Elco motors that gave it a cruising speed of 12 miles per hour. Under its raised deck forward were the galley and quarters for a crew of four. It had a

large glassed-in deckhouse, combining living and dining rooms with a forward control station that was separated from the rest of the area by brass rails.

Aft of this structure was a low cabin trunk that housed quarters for two guests, a bathroom, and owners' quarters that had a double bed and a day bed. Finally there was a large after deck that could hold six of the wicker chairs that were the nautical style of the time, being comfortable but light in weight. It was possible to walk from bow to stern on its deck. Its owner was a Detroiter, George Harrison Phelps.

In 1926, under the Hacker-Fermann name and Hacker's design, the much faster 85-foot cruiser *Rosewill* was built by Defoe. An express cruiser, driven by two V-12 Packard engines, it was one of the larger Hacker boats and one of the smaller vessels built by Defoe at that time—Defoe was now best known for yachts well over 100 feet long—and it blended fine design and fine

The 85-foot *Rosewill,* built by DeFoe Shipbuilding at Bay City, Michigan, in 1926, was one of Hacker's larger designs. It pioneered dual controls—one set in the wheelhouse–living room, one set on the bridge. © *Mystic Seaport, Rosenfeld Collection, Mystic, Connecticut*

The engine room of *Rosewill* contained two V-12 Packard engines. Between them is its Atlas generator.
© *Mystic Seaport, Rosenfeld Collection, Mystic, Connecticut*

construction. With a long raised deck forward, it was beautiful both in overall appearance and in careful detail. It had controls both on a flying bridge and in the combined wheelhouse–living room, and it had every kind of navigational equipment then known. Its interior accommodations were luxurious.

The partnership with Fermann was dissolved in 1927, though he may have continued for a short time with some of the deals already in hand. Probably Hacker bought him out of the partnership. But as with the endings of other concerns in which Hacker was involved, the details remain vague.

A Boat for the King of Siam

As mentioned earlier, Hacker refused a request from the Japanese before World War I to design

the equivalent of a PT boat, because he didn't want to become embroiled in international armaments and politics. But in 1930 his enlarged Mount Clemens factory did turn out a commuter that Hacker designed for the king of Siam. As the Mount Clemens *Monitor* announced on May 23, "His Royal Highness, Praja Dhipok, of Siam, will have classy $35,000 craft with gold radio worth $3,000 and other trimmings." The radio would be installed by the Radio Corporation of America. A similar story in the Detroit *Free Press* gave the same price. (The price of a stock 38-foot commuter was $17,000, so $35,000 was probably correct, though prices quoted elsewhere have gone as high as $100,000.)

Having an enclosed cabin on what was essentially an overgrown two-step runabout hull,

it could travel at more than a mile a minute. In descriptions, its length is often rounded off at 40 feet, but a 1930 Hackercraft advertisement says, "In this 38-foot Packard-powered Hackercraft Cruiser-Commuter, recently built in our custom department for the king of Siam, a new world's commuter record of 63.73 miles per hour was clocked by His Majesty's own representatives over a measured mile course." The boat was the same length as the only-slightly-less-elegant stock Hackercraft commuters that followed its development. The engine, however, was special. Driving through a Hacker reduction gear, it was a 650-horsepower 12-cylinder Packard said to have been designed for use in the dirigibles of the day. Not only did the king's boat have solid gold fixtures in its cabin—Hacker had two of his nieces install some of them—but it also was paid for in gold bullion when gold was $35 an ounce. The Hacker Boat Company carried its insurance with a firm called Nickel and Saph; one of the partners,

Otto Nickel, handled the transaction. (The boat still exists in the Royal Boathouse at Bangkok.)

Hacker had preceded this boat with a custom 36-footer of similar appearance, built by the Robinson Marine Construction Co., a builder of luxurious commuters. The Robinson boat had only a six-cylinder Petrel engine, and its sedan cabin ran all the way to the forward deck; it did not have the open forward cockpit with canvas top that distinguished the royal boat and the Hackercraft commuters that followed it, nor did it have their powerful engines.

As a result of enlarging the plant, the Hacker Boat Company could announce in June 1930 that it had opened a special custom department— *Lockpat II* was built there. But unhappily, the depression struck the company in 1931. Commuters suddenly went out of fashion. There would only be occasional orders from that time on.

The special Hacker commuter designed for the king of Siam, in a picture taken from a 1930 Hackercraft advertisement. This 38-footer, driven by a Packard engine of 650 horsepower, was clocked at 63.73 miles per hour. The interior cabin fittings were of solid gold, and the boat was paid for in gold bullion. It still exists in the Royal Boathouse at Bangkok. *Courtesy S. Steven McCready*

Eagles' Nest, equipped today with a Chrysler Royal straight eight, shows a good turn of speed. Such early boats were often raced informally. *Classic Boating*

Chapter Four

Conquering the Competition
Hacker Race Boats

Before the 1933 Gold Cup contest, held in Detroit that September, a small, nondescript boat named *El Lagarto* was relegated to an end slip of the dock. A spectator looked down at the two men who were with it. "You fellows racing or watching?" he asked.

"Oh, it's a nice day. We'll go out there and tag along, I guess," said George Reis, the man behind the wheel.

During the warm-up laps, the crowd was amused at this little craft "with an ungainly bouncing gait, which gave the boat the appearance of a big, friendly puppy dog." At the starting gun *El Lagarto*, ignored by the other drivers up to that point, shot across the line 25 feet ahead of the nearest boat, and none of them ever got that close to it again.

It was competing against the best boats of the day, among them Horace Dodge Jr.'s *Delphine IV,* the favorite, which had won the trophy the preceding year, and a new Dodge boat, produced for him in England by what were considered the best designers and builders. Dodge owned several other boats in the contest that year—the whole group of which Reis later referred to as "The Dodge Navy."

El Lagarto, driven by Reis, its owner, with stockbroker Dick Bowers as mechanic, stayed comfortably ahead of all the others and won the cup. During the next three years no one surpassed it. This was a sport in which old boats could sometimes survive—though seldom as long as *El Lagarto*—but also where new boats sometimes kept their winning edge for only a season or two.

Reis had two homes. The summer one was at Bolton's Landing, New York, on Lake George, where he served a term as mayor. In colder weather he retreated to Pasadena, California. He kept his boat at Lake George, but his Southwestern winters led him to choose the Spanish *El Lagarto*—The Lizard—as its name. John Hacker had designed and built the boat in 1922 as a V-bottom semidisplacement craft. Named *Miss Mary,* it was intended as a racer. The grains and colors of the wood in its hull didn't match—one of the

reasons that it looked like a poor relation to the fancier boats that were competing. (Hacker was in so many ways a perfectionist, one wonders how he let this happen.)

As *Miss Mary,* its performance had been undistinguished. A look at its races suggests that that may have been caused as much by its crew as by the boat itself. Now Gold Cup rules had changed again and the new owner was able to put a powerful—but 10-year-old—Packard 1M 621 engine in the well-designed hull. The engine was supposed to produce 300 horsepower; when Reis had finished tuning it, it produced considerably more. He also proceeded to "shingle" its bottom—adding a series of 5/8-inch steps across it, which had been forbidden to Gold Cup racers in its days as *Miss Mary.* With the shingled bottom he added air vents—a pipe on each side of the keel, through the bottom just abaft each step—an idea others had used effectively in the past. The vents relieved the air vacuum that otherwise might have held back the boat, and by controlling the pipes with shut-off valves that closed one side or the other he could turn it more nimbly.

How much credit should Hacker have for all this? The boating experts of the day praised Reis for his ingenuity, but they obviously considered that Hacker's basic form and structure were the main accomplishments. In September 1934 *Powerboating* wrote:

"The hull, designed by John L. Hacker, N.A., and built by the Hacker Boat Co., Mount Clemens, Mich., in 1923, hasn't had a single plank added to make it into a hydroplane instead of a displacement racer, as originally planned. The way the wonder boat has lasted through the years is a remarkable tribute to its builder and also to the genius of George Reis and his pal-mechanic Dick Bowers."

Today the boat is in the Adirondack Museum.

Racing Boats, 1920s

Miss Mary was only one of many Hacker boats that raced in the early 1920s. In 1920, at Miami, a runabout that

he had designed and that the owner had given the coy name of *We We,* averaged 36 miles per hour during trials, the fastest in its class—limited to marine-engined craft, which Hacker favored over aero-engined racers. During the race itself, yet another Hacker boat, *N'Everthin',* came in first with *We We* 500 feet behind. Each was powered by a 200-horsepower six-cylinder Hall-Scott engine. Other Hacker boats jousted in the various races of the year. Among them were *Snapshot, Falcon III, Sure Cure, Miss New Orleans,* and *Comanche,* the last driven by Edsel Ford. Hacker also designed *Miss Hurricane* for the Pacific Coast that year.

Hacker's early custom racers earned him good press, name recognition, and most important, more customers.

Adieu

In the February 1921 regatta in Miami, owner Webb Jay of Chicago entered the Hacker-designed runabout *Adieu* in the race for the Fisher Trophy. This was a race for displacement (or more accurately, semidisplacement) boats. *Adieu* was a V-bottom boat with a keel that had considerable rocker, so that at speed its normal 32-foot waterline became only 24 feet, much reducing the friction between hull and water.

According to *Yachting* for March 1921, "*Adieu* was the dark horse of the entries, in as much as she was a brand new boat and her capabilities were not known beforehand. She was a beautiful piece of work, of V-bottom design, 32 feet long by 6 1/2 feet beam, lightly, yet strongly built. Her power plant is a model L.M. six-cylinder, Hall-Scott motor, 5-inch by 7-inch bore and stroke, of 200 horsepower."

There were two other competitors, one of them *Rainbow,* which had won the race the previous year at Detroit. It was owned and driven by the Canadian sportsman Harry Greening, and

A 1922 Hacker "Peerless" racing runabout.
Classic Boating

was one of many boats of that name that he raced over the years. It was a 32-footer with a six-cylinder Sterling engine.

The third boat to race was *Orlo II*. Again quoting *Yachting,* it was, "a big, new sea-sled of the type developed by Albert Hickman and owned by Geo. Leary, Jr. This boat was 32 1/2 feet on the water, 37 1/2 feet overall, and she was equipped with two model G.R. dual valve Sterlings, 5 1/2-inch by 6 3/4-inch. The boat was heavy and the whole outfit weighed close to 5 1/2 tons."

The Hickman Sea Sled was essentially a catamaran with two narrow hulls joined together at the top. Sea Sleds were popular recreational boats of the day, selling mostly as outboard motor boats, but ranging in size up to 30-foot day cruisers. They used somewhat the same principle as would the later three-point racers: air and water, channeled at speed into the tunnel between the hulls, lifted them, reducing their contact with the

surface. As a result, they were reasonably fast, but the need to keep the hulls attached solidly together usually made them too heavy to race on equal terms against other boats. Because of their sturdy construction, however, they often fared better in rough water than did their lighter competitors.

On the initial day of the race, *Adieu* was first across the line at the starting gun, followed by *Rainbow* and *Orlo II*. "There followed in the next hour and a quarter one of the most consistent performances ever seen on the water. Not once did any boat falter and not once did they change positions." *Adieu* won.

On the second day, *Adieu* once again jumped away in the lead, followed by the other two in the same order as before. *Rainbow* struck a piece of driftwood that damaged its propeller and slowed it considerably. *Orlo II* continued to pursue *Adieu* until the latter slowed and stopped. *Orlo* passed it. The problem on *Adieu* was caused by a failed

The Peerless Motor Company's six-cylinder 300-horsepower Gold Cup engine of the Hacker "Peerless," one of only two such engines built. *Classic Boating*

spark plug; it was replaced and it was off again, but *Orlo II* finished ahead.

The setting of the third race was changed from sheltered water to the open sea. The boats had to run out to the starting line, and at 3 P.M., the appointed time, *Orlo* had not arrived. One of the rules of the Fisher race was that it always started on time, so *Adieu* and *Rainbow* headed off, *Adieu* again in the lead. (*Orlo II* eventually limped onto the scene, having had mechanical trouble, but did not enter the race.) For 50 miles, the two racers bumped and jumped over the seas. Toward the end, Harry Greening opened up everything that *Rainbow's* engine could produce, creeping up on *Adieu,* but Jay kept the latter ahead, crossing the line three seconds before his competitor.

Four boats raced for the Tufts-Lyon Trophy, off Los Angeles in March 1922, but it developed into a duel—with an unusual ending—between *Mystery,* owned by Frank Garbutt, and *Miss Los Angeles,* a Hacker boat owned by the actor, Dustin Farnum. At the end of the first heat, the two boats crossed the line abreast. During the second heat,

Adieu, the Hacker racer designed for the 1921 Fisher Trophy race, powered by a 200-horsepower Hall-Scott, defeated her competitors at Miami. Here she leads the second-place *Rainbow.* © *Mystic Seaport, Rosenfeld Collection, Mystic, Connecticut*

Mystery had spark plug trouble and at the end was almost a minute behind *Miss Los Angeles*.

In the third heat, after crossing the starting line, *Mystery* "swerved suddenly, apparently unmanageable, and dived under a wave," according to *Motor Boat*. "Meanwhile *Miss Los Angeles* sped around the breakwater, keeping within about 100 feet of it. Suddenly she, too, sheered and ran up on the rocks, bending one of her rudders and coming to a stop. Harry Vorhauer, driving for Mr. Farnum, and A. L. Leavitt, his mechanician, got the boat clear and going again, but the damaged rudder interfered with her speed. She made the final lap in 33:07:6, as against her fastest lap of 21:12, beating Fellows [*Fellows IV*, one of the other boats] by 24 seconds." Rather than a test of speed, this race came down to the ability of boat and crew to overcome unexpected conditions. It's not clear exactly why the boats went out of control, but the crew's ability to get *Miss Los Angeles* back into the race reflected well both on the men aboard, and in the boat's overall strength and resiliency.

Gar Wood had come to monopolize the Gold Cup races with his floating powerplants—lightly built hydroplanes that had engines of maximum size and power, usually converted from aircraft engines. A millionaire devoted to the sport, he poured almost unlimited funds into his boats. Other competitors lost interest and spectators were not drawn to contests that would have only one outcome—another Gar Wood victory. So prior to the 1922 Gold Cup race, the American Powerboat Association changed the rules, barring hydroplanes and limiting horsepower.

Miss A.P.B.A.

Hacker was able to respond with V-bottom designs. His *Arab VI*, powered by a Sterling six-cylinder 180-horsepower engine, came in second out of a Gold Cup field of 13 in 1922 and also registered the best top speed in that race, 41 miles per hour. *Motor Boating* selected him to design a boat incorporating the American Power Boat Association's new rules and published his plans for a "Speedy 26-Foot Runabout" named *Miss A.P.B.A.* in honor of the Association. "For the benefit of those who want speed and comfort without riding about in a hydroplane of excessive speed

Baby Sure Cure, powered by a 450-horsepower Liberty engine, became the fastest single-engine hydroplane when it made a lap at the 1922 Chicago Regatta at 64.8 miles per hour. The Mariners' Museum, Newport News, Virginia

possibilities," the magazine wrote, "the little displacement runabout which Mr. Hacker has designed this month will fill every requirement." The boat was powered with a 125-horsepower four-cylinder Kermath marine motor, had Hacker's usual slightly concave V-bottom, and had specifications "such as to make it eligible for competition in the Gold Cup races."

The boat could easily attain a speed of 40 miles per hour, the magazine said, but was "in all probability beyond the capability of amateur builders." A few sentences later it added, "It is hardly recommended that its construction be undertaken by other than skillful mechanics." Although the full plans were published in *Motor Boating*, the magazine also offered to provide blueprints. It noted that "Mr. Hacker is willing to furnish to builders of this boat the benefit of his skill and experience with them and cannot hope to make any promises as to the performance of this boat if unauthorized changes are made in the design."

The number of boats built to this design is unknown, but *Miss A.P.B.A.* set a standard for

the several years that those Gold Cup rules were in effect.

At that time Hacker also turned out the racer *Mystery V,* a "stepless" 25-footer driven by a 12-cylinder Liberty engine, which became the champion of the Pacific Coast.

Rainbow III

For the 1923 Gold Cup race, Hacker designed *Rainbow III* for Harry Greening. The 25-foot, 6-inch boat was built by Ditchburn in the Muskoka region of Canada, just east of Georgian Bay, and powered with a newly marketed Packard Six engine.

The race was held at Detroit. Probably Hacker took his family to the Yacht Club to see the races—his standard procedure on Labor Day. Six other boats competed. *Baby Packard*—another Hacker design—was mishandled and turned over at the start, throwing its driver-owner and mechanic into the water. *Rainbow III*, driven by Greening, won the first two heats easily. To quote the October 1923 *Yachting* magazine: "In the third race he had the event sewed up when on the

ninth lap of the 10-lap course he was seen to slow up and the mechanician was observed examining the rudder. The pin had sheered off at the bottom of the strut and while the boat went on and finished under reduced speed the best it got was a tie on points with *Packard Chriscraft*." According to the rules, if there was a tie, the cup went to the boat with the best elapsed time for all three heats—*Packard Chriscraft*. "There is no doubt

that *Rainbow III* was the best boat in the race . . . and it looks as if the system of scoring had something wrong with it."

Rainbow III was not only the best in the race, but probably the finest racing boat of its day. It brought together the racing experience of its owner and of its designer, and it was built by the leading Canadian builder. It had what had become the normal concave V-bottom hull, but

Edsel Ford's Hacker-designed *Woodfish* of 1923 was briefly the fastest semidisplacement runabout. Although it met the requirements for that class, it was basically a racing machine. It was one of the last boats Edsel raced. © *Mystic Seaport, Rosenfeld Collection, Mystic, Connecticut*

In a 1924 Buffalo race *Nick-Nack* leads *Baby Gar IV*, although the latter eventually won this race. Earlier, in a 1921 race for runabouts, *Nick Nack*, with a 200-horsepower Hall-Scott, made a record speed in that class, covering 50 miles at 41.3 miles per hour. In 1922 it won the Fisher-Allison Trophy. © *Mystic Seaport, Rosenfeld Collection, Mystic, Connecticut*

Miss Tampa, in the Gold Cup race of 1925, broke a rudder strut in the second heat and had to fall out, but even so took second place in a field of nine. Here it is at Miami in 1926 in a race for boats of the Gold Cup Class, which it won. © *Mystic Seaport, Rosenfeld Collection, Mystic, Connecticut*

with a slightly narrower transom than usual, to cut down the drag of water moving past the hull.

Racing engines ran on a mixture of 35 to 50 percent benzol with high-test gasoline. The benzol prevented instant detonation of the fuel and smoothed the burning, somewhat like the lead that was later used in gasoline for cars. The boat's 1M-618 Packard Gold Cup Six of 225 horsepower used just such a mixture.

Its propeller was placed some distance aft of the transom in order to be free of the currents passing around the hull. The best manganese bronze rudders often were bent by the force of water when a fast boat turned. On this boat the rudder was made of flexible saw steel, copper plated, and the underwater supports of the rudder and the nickel steel propeller shaft were combined.

Greening took the boat back to the Muskoka Lakes and made a distance record with it there, running 1,064 miles in 24 hours. In

1926 at Miami Beach, *Miss Tampa,* a boat of Hacker's design, won a race for the Gold Cup class boats. Second was *Palm Beach Days,* the renamed *Rainbow III.*

Rainbow III's outstanding performance in the 1923 Gold Cup obscured the accomplishment of another Hacker boat, Edsel Ford's *Woodfish,* which in a different race of that same regatta won the Seibert Trophy, and also became for a time the fastest semidisplacement boat in the world. Hacker advertised it as a runabout—although it was purely a racing machine—perhaps in part because the control station was in the front cockpit, which actually was nearly amidships. Its engine was well aft under a curved hood, and the mechanic rode just behind it in a stern cockpit.

Ford, however, was losing his interest in boat racing, growing more important in the auto industry, and becoming more distant. Twice Hacker wrote to him, once in 1926 and again in 1933, suggesting enthusiastically that he build a

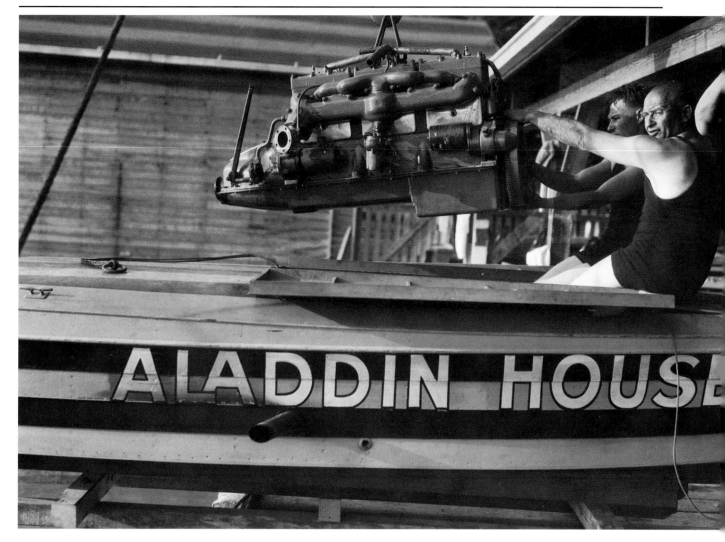

Aladdin Houses, one of the Biscayne Baybies, has its engine installed. Eleven Biscayne Baybies were built by the Purdy Boat Company after the developers of Palm Beach commissioned Hacker to design a small, one-design class of racers. The developers named the boats Biscayne Baybies. Each was 21 feet long and was powered by a six-cylinder 100-horsepower Scripps engine. The boats first raced in 1925. © *Mystic Seaport, Rosenfeld Collection, Mystic, Connecticut*

new Gold Cup racer. Each time the very short answering letter starts, "Mr. Ford appreciates your letter of . . . but. . . ." The 1926 reply's typed signature, presumably below a written one, is simply "Office of Edsel B. Ford." That of 1933 is at least "Secretary to Edsel B. Ford." At one time Edsel Ford and John Hacker were on friendly terms; these politely chilly rebuffs from Ford's subordinates ended that relationship.

One-Design Racers, 1925–1926

In the mid-1920s the developers of Palm Beach and of Tampa, striving to put their new cities on the map, commissioned Hacker to design two new one-design motor racing classes called, respectively, the Biscayne Baybies and the Tampa Baybies. (Don't blame Hacker for the cutesy names invented by the promoters; in use they soon became plain Babies.) These boats were 21 feet long and had engines under 340 cubic inches, fitting them for what were known as the Junior Gold Cup Races, more formally called contests for the Duff-Greening Trophy—a race under Gold Cup rules but for smaller craft. They also of course raced among themselves throughout the season.

The Biscayne Babies first raced in 1925. The Purdy Boat Company built 11 of them to Hacker's design, each powered by a six-cylinder, 100-horsepower Scripps engine. The regatta organizers wanted to introduce the one-design class with the maximum flourish, so they enlisted Carl Fisher. In addition to being the

major developer of Palm Beach, Fisher was a powerboat enthusiast and owner of the Indianapolis 500 auto racetrack. He enrolled 11 well-known professional auto racing drivers to handle the boats. None of them had ever driven a racing boat before, but they were given two days to familiarize themselves with their charges. A representative of Scripps had tuned all of the engines so that they ran equally well. The race was run in six 12-mile heats—all were fast and furious. The spectators enjoyed an exciting show. The winning boat was *Hialeah,* driven by Louis Chevrolet, a famous auto racer after which the well-known automobile line was named.

Tampa put forth a great effort to promote itself in 1926, staging its first regatta which, *The Rudder* magazine commented, insured that "in the future Tampa must be considered as one of the racing centers of the Southland." A number of racing classes participated, the 10 Tampa Babies among them. Tampa introduced their Babies with considerably less panache than had Palm Beach, however. They first were turned over to visiting yachtsmen to have an informal race. (Hacker, driving one of them, came in fourth.) They were used for a women's race. Then they were given to a group of local newspapermen for a contest

within that profession. Unlike Palm Beach, the Tampa organizers seemed unsure of how much and what type of attention to give the event. As a result, their boats were never as successful as the Biscayne Babies.

In 1927 *The Rudder* reported on another successful event in Palm Beach: "As usual, the Biscayne Baybies put up mighty fine racing. These sporty little craft, powered with Scripps engines, are about the most successful one-design power racers in America."

The Lady Helens

Hacker designed other boats especially for the Junior Gold Cup races, most notably *Lady Helen I* and *Lady Helen II.* These two boats must have given the designer-builder an outlet for some of his more unusual ideas. *Lady Helen (I),* built in 1924, was a lapstrake boat—something that seems almost alien to the Hacker inspiration, though he created others, among them *Curtiss Wilgold,* a sweepstakes racer. The new *Lady* was "a trim little 21-foot clinker-built craft powered with a six-cylinder 'Junior Gold Cup' Scripps motor," according to *Yachting* of October 1924, which also said of the race at Detroit, in which it was driven by Dick Locke, that "all three heats were easily won by *Lady Helen.*"

Again at Detroit, this time in 1926, *Lady Helen II* made its appearance—and quite an appearance it was. Said *Motor Boat* that September, "It is a low freeboard craft of interesting type, with an odd hood over its Miller motor, the whole effect being enhanced by gold paint over the entire boat above water." *Lady Helen II*, driven by Dick Locke, won, with *Lady Helen I* coming in second.

Later in 1926 the two boats competed at Washington, D.C., during the regatta held for the President's Cup, in what was termed the "Junior President's Cup," a race with a single 9-mile heat. It was a Hacker race. The winner was *Lady Helen II*, followed by four Biscayne Babies, with *Lady Helen I* coming in last.

When he watched a race, Hacker usually had a stopwatch in his hand and an abstracted expression. People who saw him said, only half-jokingly, that he was already designing the next racer in his mind. His attitude toward races was philosophical: There were a thousand and one things that could go wrong; if they didn't happen, his boat would win.

The Spitfires

A 1927 Hacker catalog showed fewer stock boats than custom ones. Among the racers included were *Kitty Hawk*, "First 50-mile hydroplane in America, first to have propeller aft of transom"; *Oregon Kid*, "The Modern Hydroplane . . . Defeated all hydroplanes 1913 and 1914"; *Hawk*

In addition to the Baybies, Hacker designed similar boats for the Junior Gold Cup races— run under Gold Cup rules, but for smaller craft. The winner in 1924 was his *Lady Helen*, a 21-footer powered by a Scripps Junior Gold Cup 6. © *Mystic Seaport, Rosenfeld Collection, Mystic, Connecticut*

Eye, "First 60-mile hydroplane in America"; *Sure Cure,* "First hydroplane to make over 65 miles an hour"; *Rainbow III,* "First displacement racer of narrow stern and outboard rudder type"; *Yankee Doodle,* "Said to have made the greatest speed of its size to date"; and *Miss Tampa, Adieu, Nick Nack,* the *Lady Helens,* and the *Spitfires.*

The *Spitfires* were a recent development. For the editors of *Power Boating,* Hacker designed a small racing hydroplane in the 151-ci (engine capacity) class. The plans were published for general use in the magazine in March of 1926. Hacker's versatility is shown here: The man who designed the 85-foot cruiser *Rosewill* also was asked to design the smallest sized inboard racing boat—and did it well. The new class was called the Pelican, but that name was soon obscured by boats of the Pelican class that were named Spitfire.

An eager racer obtained a set of plans from Hacker before they were published in the magazine. He was the Buffalo millionaire and boat lover, James H. Rand Jr. He entered his boat, *Spitfire IV,* in the Tampa Regatta early in 1926, where it made a new small-boat record of 40.6 miles per hour, and he looked forward to racing it in the Buffalo Regatta the coming summer.

The Rudder later said of Rand (in November 1927), "His boats range all the way from the big power yacht *Spitfire* down to a handful of tiny outboards. All of his boats are named *Spitfire* and to tell them apart he has added prefixes, suffixes and all manner of words, initials and numerals, but it is still claimed that he has to maintain a card index system to keep track of them."

The new 151 was named *Spitfire IV.* He entered it in class in the Buffalo Regatta of August 12 and 15, 1926. It won the first heat easily, but after crossing the finish line at high speed, it capsized—for reasons not explained—throwing him into the water. He was fished out undamaged, but the boat was badly smashed.

Though it is unlikely that he planned to capsize, he had another hull waiting in the Richardson boatbuilding plant in the Buffalo suburb of North Tonawanda. The remains of *Spitfire IV* were lugged to Richardson's, its Fronty marine engine was hoisted out and lowered into the new hull under supervision of a Fronty Motor Company representative, and after a long night's work, *Spitfire V* emerged, ready to compete in—and win—the race. (*Motor Boating* commented that a *Spitfire VI* was also waiting offstage in case of further mishaps. Rand was a careful planner.)

Mrs. Rand wanted a boat to enter the 1927 race for the Duke of York's Trophy in England.

On the boat's sign:

HACKER·BUILT
151 Class Hydroplane
Speed 41 to 44 Miles Per Hour
Designed for every type of service
Complete Plans made by the
C Mack Power Boating
Hacker & Fermann · Detroit, Mich.

Spitfire V was renamed *Little Spitfire* and transferred to her ownership. For this race the boat was equipped with a supercharged eight-cylinder Miller engine. Ralph Snoddy of Los Angeles went as the driver. The boat easily won each of the 30-nautical-mile heats at Southampton.

Back came *Little Spitfire* to the United States. The *Detroit News* had offered a cup for an international race at that city and in response, there was what *Motor Boat* called a "foreign invasion" of two English and two German boats in September of 1927. *Little Spitfire* and one other from the U.S. were entered; the other boat soon pulled out because of mechanical trouble. The Hacker-designed *Little Spitfire* won easily,

"and its competitors probably do not yet know how fast it really traveled," said *Motor Boat*.

With its larger engine, *Little Spitfire* could no longer race in the 151 Class. But Rand, perhaps enjoying any confusion he caused, entered—and won—the 151 race at that same Detroit Regatta with a Hacker-designed *Miss Spitfire V.*

The Rands continued to race their boats. At the San Diego Winter Regatta in 1928, *Miss Spitfire V,* whose owner was listed as Marian H. Rand, won in its class handily. The driver, Ralph Snoddy, reached a record speed of 55.42 miles per hour.

Hacker's other boats continued to acquit themselves well. In the Buffalo Regatta of July

A hydroplane of the 151 racing class of 1926, of which Hacker designed and built many. The boat design was named Pelican, but the class was dominated by boats named *Spitfire*. The Mariners' Museum, Newport News, Virginia'

Little Spitfire, a
Hacker Spitfire
converted by
installing an eight-
cylinder Miller
engine, won the
Duke of York's
Trophy in England
in 1927. Returning
to the United
States, it won an
international race
at Detroit.
© *Mystic Seaport,
Rosenfeld
Collection, Mystic,
Connecticut.*

1928, *Curtis Wilgold* came in first in the Gold
Cup class, "an easy winner." In 1928 Hacker
brought out another 151 boat, this one in the
"unlimited" class, meaning that the owner could
tune the boat's engine in any way he wished.
The aggressive little one-man boat named,
appropriately, *Sparrow*, had a Miller engine. It
won in 1928 at Newport, driven by its owner,
Elmer Johnson. In April 1929, at Palm Beach,
"Commodore Johnson, *Sparrow* and he, made a
nose dive for the bottom of Lake Worth." But in
August 1929 at Red Bank, according to *Yachting*
that October, "Elmer H. Johnson drove the
Hacker-designed *Sparrow* to victory in all three
heats of the 151 class, unlimited."

Other Hacker boats wove their way through
the race meetings in which *Sparrow* performed.

At Palm Beach in 1929, according to *The Rudder*
that April, "One of the prettiest races of the
regatta was the one between the runabouts. The
first heat was for five miles, and *Adriatic*, a Hacker
runabout with a new 200-horsepower Kermath,
walked away with the honors." It did so in the
other heats as well. In Miami in 1931 a
200-horsepower Sterling-powered Hackercraft
named *Musketeer II,* owned by A. H. Howell, won
both its heats against seven competitors.

A Harmsworth Racer, 1928

For the 1928 Harmsworth International
Race—the one dominated by Gar Wood's high-
powered craft—Hacker designed a racer that was
quite different from anything seen before. It was
made for James Talbot of Los Angeles, was named

A second *Miss Los Angeles,* designed by Hacker to compete in the Harmsworth International Race of 1928. The hull was two-ply veneer and the three-step bottom was covered with a quarter-inch rubber surface. It was powered by two 1,000-horsepower Miller engines, in which the cylinders were arranged in three banks of eight each, the center one vertical, the others at 45-degree angles. It could easily reach 70 miles per hour, but had an unfortunate tendency to turn over. The unusual craft was restored by Bill Morgan, builder of current Hacker boats, and is now in the Antique Boat Museum, Clayton, New York. *The Mariners' Museum, Newport News, Virginia*

Miss Los Angeles II, and was to be driven by Ralph Snoddy. It was powered by two 24-cylinder Miller engines of 1,000 horsepower each; the cylinders were arranged in three banks of eight, the center one vertical, the others at 45-degree angles to the vertical. The hull was of two-ply veneer and the bottom, which had three steps, was covered with a quarter-inch composition rubber surface. It also carried a slightly concave V shape all of the way aft. The boat was fast; in trials with it, Snoddy reached 70 miles per hour.

On August 1, 1928, the *Mount Clemens Daily Leader* reported that Snoddy was at the Hacker plant tuning up the boat. Confusing the *Spitfires* as did many others, the paper noted that the preceding year Snoddy had piloted *Miss Spitfire* to a win in a somewhat more limited international race. (That boat actually was *Little Spitfire.*) Gar Wood had also intended to compete

there, but his boat struck a steamer's swell and turned over shortly before the event, so he could not race. "If bad luck does not once more step in to interfere with his plans, Snoddy this year will have his chance to compete with Gar Wood for the all-American driving championship."

In October 1928 *The Rudder,* reporting on the Harmsworth held in September of that year, commented "*Miss Los Angeles,* the slippery sided, rubber soled affair from the Pacific Coast, was all primed to give Gar Wood a real race in the second heat, but things happened quickly, and soon after crossing the starting line the boat from out west was seen to be floating bottom up with its crew nonchalantly waving to the crowds along the shore." The bad luck this time had plagued Snoddy.

Miss Los Angeles II was evidently very unstable. In a later race it turned turtle again, and that largely ended its career. (The unusual boat has

Ethyl-Ruth IV, a handsome Hacker racer of 1934 whose owner gave it little chance to show its capabilities. In its one race for the Gold Cup, it started late and soon fell out from trouble with its Miller engine. One of Hacker's streamlined hulls, it has been preserved and restored and has become a symbol of its era, in 1999 being displayed at a Paris exhibition of "retro-mobile" cars and boats. © *Mystic Seaport, Rosenfeld Collection, Mystic, Connecticut*

been restored by Bill Morgan, the current owner of the Hacker trademark, and is now in the Antique Boat Museum at Clayton, New York.)

Gold Cup Boats, 1930s

In January 1933 Hacker wrote his second letter to Edsel Ford, suggesting that he underwrite a new Gold Cup boat to which Hacker would give his full attention—"I have plenty of time right now." As this was the depths of the depression, that would certainly be true. Why would Hacker write to Edsel again after his 1926 approach had been so snubbed? His two-page letter seems overdone, and one senses a certain desperation. Edsel turned down this second approach.

El Lagarto emerged from obscurity in 1933. The noted racing driver William Horn, in an interview published in the April 1936 *Yachting,* commented:

"A boat might kill me but she never will lick me. That is why George Reis is so successful with *El Lagarto.* That old lizard is going to fly into a thousand pieces one of these days, but George never thinks of that. He gives his boat hell and pushes her for all she's worth when he has to. He is utterly fearless."

El Lagarto never flew apart like that, thanks to Hacker's construction, but the passage shows the single-minded and fatalistic attitude of a successful racing driver.

To further understand the experience of racers in the Gold Cup class at that time—the strains on crew and equipment, the skill, the luck—it helps to read a description by Charles Griffin, who had been the mechanic for the Dodge entry *Delphine IV* in the President's Cup Race against *El Lagarto.* It appeared in the November 1934 *Motor Boating.*

Just before the Cup race began, *Delphine IV* struck a piece of wood and bent its propeller:

"The starting gun! Our start is terribly late. Down the stretch to the first turn we go. We get boxed in on the way down, and get hosed down beautifully by *Louisa* and *El Lagarto.* I cannot see, or catch my breath except in gasps, for a quarter of a lap. We're running in fourth position. The rest of that heat is history. We finished third. *Hornet* was wrecked trying to pass *El Lagarto. Arctic Tern* capsized. *El Lagarto* won!"

(The hosing down was from the flying spray and wash of the other boats.) In the second heat of that race, *Delphine IV* was running smoothly in the lead when the engine made a "heavy sound of steel against steel," as though the crankshaft and a

connecting rod had let go—and they were out of the race. Again *El Lagarto* won.

A designer's best efforts could be blunted not only by the luck of the race, but also by mechanical and human problems, especially those of owners and drivers of his race boats. Consider

John L. Hacker watching a race at Detroit. © *Mystic Seaport*, Rosenfeld Collection, Mystic, Connecticut

Ethyl-Ruth IV, which was entered in the 1934 Gold Cup race on Lake George. Said *Powerboating* that September:

"*Ethyl-Ruth* made a belated start. . . . She is an exceptionally beautiful craft, probably the finest looking boat in the Gold Cup class. She planes beautifully and runs smoothly with but little fuss. Designed by John L. Hacker, N. A., and built by the Hacker Boat Co., Mount Clemens, Mich., she is powered with a 16-cylinder Miller engine and seems to have as much speed as any of the other boats but she didn't have a chance to show it."

Arriving late at the starting line when the other boats had almost finished their first lap, it was driven wide open for two laps in an attempt to catch them—and its engine blew up. It was towed from the course.

It did not compete for the Gold Cup in 1935. In 1936 *Yachting,* looking forward to the Gold Cup race that lay ahead, commented, "John Shibe, Philadelphia baseball magnate, had entered *Ethyl Ruth IV* but withdrew her later on the grounds that the new opposed cylinder engine that Harry Miller was building for him would not be completed. However, Mr. Shibe is unpredictable. He may turn up with his big Hacker-built hull and astonish everyone by going somewhere with it." He did not. The boat was never in another Gold Cup race.

Hacker stock boats continued to do well in runabout races. Jack Rutherford, whose summer home was on Long Island and whose winter home was at Palm Beach, had raced in almost every meet along the Atlantic Coast. His wife, Maud, often accompanied him, if she was not driving a racing boat on her own. In the Around Manhattan Race in 1934, in a Kermath-powered Hackercraft, they came in first in Class I, with an average speed of 42.05 miles per hour.

The 225-Cubic-Inch Class

The 151-ci class gradually died, at least partly because some of its owners began to spend unlimited money on their boats and the others could not keep up. In time John Hacker suggested that another class be started with strict limitations, though with larger engines—the 225 class. He suggested that using marine conversions of auto engines or existing marine engines and building a 16-foot hydroplane to contain them would cost $1,200 or $1,500, and so lead to a revival of small inboard boat racing.

He took the idea to the American Power Boat Association and received the approval of its Racing

Commission. They decided that the engines could cost no more than $700. The hulls were to have a waterline length of not less than 15 1/2 feet and beam, at the widest section, of not less than 4 1/2 feet. Two-person crews were required. Races began in 1934.

Two years previously Hacker had been approached by the Canadian boatbuilder Tom Greavette, and two of Greavette's customers—the father-and-son team of Ernest and Harold Wilson— to build a small hydroplane runabout in which the younger Wilson could race on the Muskoka Lakes and other local waters. That boat, *Little Miss Canada II,* was produced in 1932, the same year that Harold, studying mechanical engineering at Toronto University, met another student, "a cute little blonde" named Lorna Reid. That summer Lorna joined the Wilson Racing Team as mechanic for the new boat.

Greavette and Hacker knew each other. In 1933 they agreed that Hacker would design exclusively for Greavette in Canada. Up to that point, Hacker had designed for others in Muskoka. The change probably did little to improve Hacker's income—the number of boats

built in the Muskokas by any builder was small compared with U.S. production—but it was a definite coup for Greavette.

Ernest Wilson, a highly successful Canadian businessman, was constantly propelling his son forward. When he learned of the new class of 225 hydroplanes, he commissioned Hacker and Greavette to provide such a boat for the 1934 season. *Little Miss Canada III* was the most powerful boat Harold had driven, and his father had signed him up for the International Trophy Race, to be held at Toronto in September. The boat was completed and was tried out by Harold and Lorna that summer. Then it was taken to Toronto, where Greavette and a technician from the Ford Motor Company, which had provided the engine, hovered over it. The race was held in open Lake Ontario, outside the harbor, each of three heats running five laps for a total of 15 miles. Seven boats from Canada and the United States competed.

In the first heat of the first important race he had ever run, Wilson was first over the starting line, and he managed to keep ahead of *Emancipator,* driven by millionaire sportsman— and experienced race driver—Mortimer Auerbach

from Atlantic City. *Little Miss Canada III* crossed the finish line first by a few seconds. But next day on the second heat Wilson and Reid felt an especially hard bump and their boat slowed down, letting Auerbach finish first. They came in second. Back at their pit they lifted the boat out of the water and found that the propeller was bent, apparently by something they had hit. They had no spare. But Ernest Wilson, ever resourceful and well placed, phoned the propeller manufacturer in Detroit and had a duplicate flown to Toronto by special plane.

Before the next heat, a fellow competitor who had ended up well back in the field, Al Swartziger of New York, showed up at the Wilson pit carrying a parcel that contained his own propeller. He offered it to Harold Wilson, who of course was able to say that they had obtained a spare—but he remembered the generous offer for the rest of his life.

In the third and final heat, Auerbach and Wilson both headed for the final marker buoy. Legally, Auerbach could pass inside the buoy, but he forgot. Wilson headed as close to the marker as he could and Auerbach, foreseeing only a crash between the boats, slacked off and fell back. Wilson and Reid won.

Little Miss Canada IV, a champion 225-ci racer built in Canada by Greavette in 1934, was designed by Hacker, who originated the 225 racing class. Because the mechanic, who was the driver's fiancée, weighed so much less than the driver, Hacker put them in separate cockpits to preserve the balance of the boat. *Courtesy Muskoka Lakes Museum*

Maybe, a restored 1936 E-Class racing runabout by Hacker. These boats were limited to engines of no more than 230-ci capacity. *Classic Boating*

Despite Hacker's original intent of making the 225s a one-design class, the owners were hard at work improving it, though within its stated limitations. The Wilsons turned again to Hacker for a *Little Miss Canada IV.* It turned out to be more refined than the previous boat, its wetted area smaller when it planed, its outside smoother. Its most obvious change was that instead of seating driver and mechanic side by side, this boat had two cockpits, one behind the other. The larger, forward, one was for the driver; the smaller, after one, for the mechanic. Hacker felt that the difference in Harold's and Lorna's weights—225

pounds versus 118—could affect the balance of the craft if they sat side by side.

The 1935 race again turned out to be a duel between Auerbach, in his new *Emancipator,* and Wilson, in his new *Little Miss Canada IV.* Again Wilson won the first, Auerbach the second heat. During the third, one problem of the tandem seating became critical. Lorna, unable to speak normally to Harold, kept him posted by shouting to him over his shoulder. As the boat headed toward the final buoy, she called out something that ended in "gaining." Taking that to be the signal that *Emancipator* was making a move to pass, Wilson

The 18-foot
E-Class *Maybe*,
of Hacker design,
raced in New
York's Finger Lakes
for many years.
Classic Boating

unwisely opened the throttle wide just as they rode up the face of a wave. The boat leaped off the wave and into the trough—becoming a submarine. But it came out the other side of the next wave, wet but still going strong. The kayaklike cockpits had prevented water from entering the hull, and the air intakes for the engine faced backward so the engine was not choked off. They made the final turn and sped down the last stretch to victory.

In October 1935, two years after the 225 class first appeared, *Motor Boating*, under the heading "AMERICA'S GREATEST RACING CLASS," trumpeted: "The 225s are already America's

greatest racing boats. To date 38 boats of this class have been built and registered with the Racing Commission of the American Power Boat Association. Many more are under construction."

A report in *Power Boating* that November commented on the President's Cup races held on the Potomac: "Despite the fact that the Gold Cup class boats were competing for the big prize of the regatta, the President's Cup, the little fellows of the rapidly coming 225 class, really stole the show. As one spectator remarked, 'It's a savage little class.'"

Hacker's vision had triumphed, and his brainchildren were running away with the sport.

Bootlegger, a restored Hackercraft 24-footer of 1936. Designed by Hacker, the boat was built by the Hacker Boat Company after he no longer owned it. ***Classic Boating***

Chapter Five

Surviving the Storm

Hacker in the Depression and War Years

On December 31, 1934, the board of the Hacker Boat Company accepted the surrender to the company of all shares of stock held by John L. Hacker and his son, John A. Hacker, "in payment of his indebtedness to the company."

As the company consisted of the two Hackers and the two McCreadys, this meant that all the Hackers' shares were surrendered to the McCreadys.

The exact reasons are not known. The McCreadys had provided the money for expanding the Mount Clemens plant. Hacker, whose commercial acumen was meager, had not realized the danger of boom-time overexpansion—but then, obviously, neither had the McCreadys. Had they grown tired of their unbusinesslike designer and decided to foreclose? Did S. Dudley McCready, the company manager, covet the title of president? Did he crave full control?

There is a further possibility. Oral history has brought down to us a picture of a John L. Hacker who by that time was saddled with heavy debts. The McCreadys may have been afraid that one of his other creditors could seize his Hacker Boat Company shares in payment of an outside indebtedness. A new, strange stockholder would certainly limit the McCreadys' control. And in those circumstances, an outsider probably would be looking more for cash repayment than mere paper stock, and could bring the company tumbling down in order to sell off the pieces.

At the same time that they accepted Hacker's stock, putting an end to his ownership, the McCreadys renewed the agreement binding him to design no other boats that competed with Hackercraft. He could "engage in the business of designing and building of boats of the class known as 'cruisers' (being boats with sleeping quarters) or boats in excess of 28 feet in length and, special custom or racing boats." Thus he was barred from designing the popular sizes of stock runabouts for anyone else and remained the captive designer for the company. Yet he was removed from management and no longer would supervise the building of his boats.

A company document dated January 2, 1935, records S. Dudley McCready's election to president and Roberta McCready's election as secretary by "the remaining directors." (Roberta was married to S. Dudley.) The 1935 Mount Clemens Directory shows S. D. McCready as the Hacker Boat Company's president and treasurer, C. P. McCready quietly remaining as vice president, and Roberta McCready as secretary.

There is little doubt that without the McCreadys the company would not have survived. Whether Hacker had to be banished is an unresolved question.

Whatever the circumstances, Hacker could scarcely be happy. He had been hailed as the world's foremost designer of fast pleasure boats, boats that were called singularly beautiful and that were known all over the world. That now meant little. The McCreadys softened the blow slightly by allowing him to continue using his office at the plant, though he largely retreated to another office that he established on East Jefferson Avenue in Detroit. His reputation was such that he soon had clients coming to his new location—though barely enough to scrape out a living. For the rest of his life he remained bitter about the loss of his company.

Hackercraft advertisements in 1935 were obviously responding to the depression. They offered 17- and 19-foot runabouts and 17- and 19-foot utilities, both designed by John L. Hacker. In large, bold-faced letters the ads said, "Priced As Low As $975."

The 225-Cubic-Inch Class, 1934

Hacker had been outstandingly successful in launching the 225-ci racing class, though in later years he regretted that the boats had not remained the simple, limited-cost racers he had envisioned. But by this time he had designed several of the boats, in addition to his *Little Miss Canadas.* Two of them, *Riptide* and *Wilmer II,* did especially well in 225 contests in the United States.

S. Dudley McCready and Roberta McCready in a 1935 19-foot Hacker runabout, a boat made in response to the Great Depression. In early January of that year, they became president and secretary, respectively, of the Hacker Boat Company. *Courtesy S. Steven McCready*

Harold Wilson and his fiancée, Lorna Reid, who raced the Hacker-designed *Little Miss Canada IV*, remained the leaders in Canada, and the international champions of the 225 class. In the late summer of 1934, they were invited to a 225 class race in the United States, at the regatta of the Baltimore Yacht Club on the Patapsco River. Although there were mild complications in arranging a chaperone for Lorna, who as usual was the Wilson riding mechanic, those were soon resolved.

The Wilson boat crossed the starting line a few feet behind the leader. Shortly the course narrowed, going under a bridge, and Wilson had to pull in behind the other boat. As he did, "a great wall of water" struck and blinded him and his mechanic, but they got through the bridge arch without hitting it and found themselves in the lead. Lap after lap they stayed ahead, noticing

some excitement every time they passed the starting barge. After receiving the checkered flag and pulling in, they were signaled to the barge. "Did you see what happened at the bridge on the first lap?" the officials asked. "Where did that lead boat go?" responded Wilson. The lead boat had hit a heavy cross swell just before the bridge, flown into the air, and done a back flip. Blinded by the water thrown up, Wilson and Reid had passed right under the flipping boat, missing it by inches before it landed upside down on the water behind them.

Then the Wilsons and *Little Miss Canada* were invited to compete in the 225 class at the President's Cup regatta at Washington. After trailering their boat there, they were disconcerted to find that their race was scheduled for Saturday and Sunday. As good Torontonians of their day— the city was known as Toronto the Good—they

balked at nonreligious Sunday activities. They dutifully raced on Saturday, coming in first in that heat, but then closed down and left.

That was the preliminary of their moving on to a Gold Cup Class boat also designed by John L. Hacker.

At home, according to Hacker's daughter Marion, "we had to live with a father who was forever alternating between elation and depression, depending on his business, in the depression years especially." He worked evenings and on weekends. He went to as many as five movies a week, especially to see the newsreels—something that today could be done much more easily with television, but that would not take him out of a household that he evidently found smothering. "He never complained about caring for us, never dreamed of leaving what *he* considered a poor marriage." He went for long walks every night;

sometimes in bad weather the police would want to bring him home. During that time, Marion often would go with him. When he was home he would play the piano, doing the pieces he had committed to memory. "Basically Papa was a simple man, living for his family, and enjoying the company of the large Hacker family [his many brothers and sisters and their children] throughout his life."

Rich clients did not always pay promptly. As Christmas approached Hacker would remind a member of some recent boat-buyer's staff that money should be forthcoming, and would wait for a response. "All in all, we had a magnificent Christmas, considering we did not know until Friday that we could have one. We purchased gifts on the 23rd, then bought the tree, and then began gift-wrapping."

A winning 225-ci racer of Hacker's design, *Riptide*, showing its stepped bottom. The 225 Class was Hacker's creation. In later years he regretted that it had not continued as a strictly limited-cost class, but it was highly popular with boat racers and spectators.
© *Mystic Seaport, Rosenfeld Collection, Mystic, Connecticut*

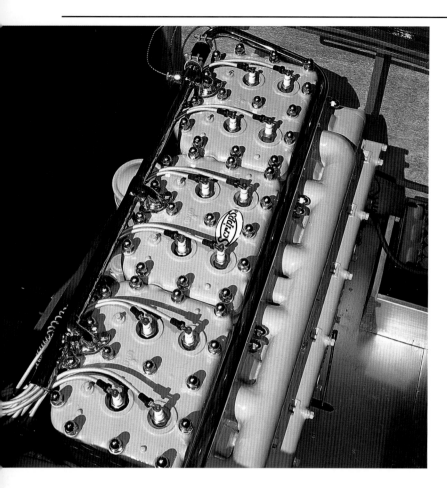

The engine of *Bootlegger,* a six-cylinder Scripps. *Classic Boating*

The Gold Cup Class, 1936–1938

In the period of the depression and the pre–World War II years, John L. Hacker did not do much with the larger racing boats, and what he did was hardly up to standard. Prior to the 1938 Gold Cup race, the new *Notre Dame II,* designed and driven by Clell Perry and known to be difficult to handle, flipped over during a trial run, sending a seriously injured Perry to the hospital. The boat was recovered and John Hacker was asked to tame its wilder characteristics. He redesigned its bottom. In the Gold Cup race in 1939, with a new driver, it dropped out because of mechanical troubles. At the President's Cup race later that year, it came in second. It still was twitchy to control, however, and its owner retired it at the end of that season and started on a new boat—but not one designed by Hacker.

Hacker's most frustrating racing craft of the period was probably the new Gold Cup boat that he designed for the racing Wilsons, father and son, Ernest and Harold, when they became tired of racing the 225s.

Harold's parents spent some time in California in the winter of 1934–1935. There Ernest met

George Reis, the owner-driver of the famous Hacker boat *El Lagarto,* and became enthusiastic about Gold Cup racing. Harold—who still was in college—was entered without his knowledge as a Gold Cup driver and John Hacker was set to work designing a new Gold Cupper, *Miss Canada II.*

The Gold Cup class was in a state of change and confusion. By 1930 most of these boats had shingled V-bottoms, though others were designed as hydroplanes. They were powered by Wright or Packard engines that may have been new, but that were of designs dating back to World War I; their owners altered and tuned them to produce maximum power—at maximum strain on the working parts. In 1935 only five boats were entered. The engine of one destroyed itself in trials the day before the race, and of the four that started, only two finished, the winner being *El Lagarto.* The Gold Cup boats seemed to be dinosaurs. It was not surprising that the feisty little 225s were stealing the show.

Perhaps Ernest Wilson had been advised to find a different engine for his Gold Cupper. The limits on engine size had been raised for the coming season; the elder Wilson had met Harry Miller, builder of racing car engines, and had commissioned him to build a 1,000-horsepower engine for the new Wilson boat. Maybe *Miss Canada II* would show the way for future Gold Cup boats.

But the story of *Miss Canada II* shows how many things—including one of Hacker's less successful designs—could go wrong with a racing craft.

The hydroplane took shape in the Greavette shop at Gravenhurst, Ontario, in the spring and early summer of 1936. The Miller engine, being made in Butler, Pennsylvania, would, according to Miller, be ready as soon as the hull was completed. It did arrive at Greavette's as the finishing touches were being made to the boat—but it came as crate loads of unassembled parts. With it came Miller and two helpers, who set to work putting it together. By late June it was fairly well assembled except for things such as supercharger, magnetos, and wiring manifold, which lurked in their shipping crates and still had to be attached. The motor was fitted into the boat and taken out again several times. By the time they had to go off to Lake George, site of the next Gold Cup race, it still had not been started.

Miller assured the Wilsons that he would finish the engine at Lake George before the race. Off they all went, Lorna with the necessary chaperone. They arrived the afternoon before the race. Next

Miss Canada II, a Hacker Gold Cup design of 1937, had the double-cockpit arrangement that he thought necessary when Harold Wilson drove and his fiancée, Lorna Reid, was mechanic—otherwise, Hacker felt, the difference in their weights might destroy the balance. The boat was fast, once the Miller engine worked properly, but not sturdy enough to withstand pounding in rough water.
© *Mystic Seaport, Rosenfeld Collection, Mystic, Connecticut*

morning, half an hour before the start, Miller announced that the engine was ready, and the boat was put into the water. Harold Wilson got in; after a couple of tries the engine started. Wilson got the boat up to 60 miles per hour—when there was a smell of burning rubber, followed by a series of backfires, and the engine stopped. *Miss Canada II* was towed in and the engine compartment was opened. The intake manifold had come loose and the entire manifold system would have to be rebuilt. No race for *Miss Canada II.*

Even though it had a new engine, the Wilson boat became one of the statistics that reflected mainly the behavior of Wright and Packard engines of ancient design. Nine contenders were entered in

that race. Before it began seven of them had wrecked their engines. Of the two starters, one dropped out after two laps and the remaining boat, *Impshi,* did a solo for the remainder of the 90-mile run.

The Wilson racing crew went home, towing the boat, while Miller and his men took the engine back to Butler, Pennsylvania. It was put back in the hull again as the boat was en route to Washington later that season to compete for the President's Cup. There *Miss Canada II* started out briskly, but on the third lap there was again the smell of burning rubber, backfiring, and then a stopped engine that could not be restarted. After the boat was towed back to the pits and the engine hatches opened, the crew saw that the hose connections between the 12 cylinders and the intake manifold had melted under the heat of the engine, so that pieces of hose and the clamps that held them in place were rattling around in the V of the engine.

This time the Wilsons took the engine home with them and hired two mechanics, one of them a skilled machinist, to work on it over the winter and to be sure that it was in running condition when it went back into the boat. Next year the Wilsons and *Miss Canada II* headed off to the cup races to be held on Labor Day in Detroit.

Hacker had designed the boat with two cockpits, just as he had done with the *Little Miss Canadas*, believing that if Harold and Lorna sat side by side, as driver and mechanic normally did, the difference in their weights would spoil the balance of the boat. The two cockpits just fitted Harold and Lorna. Then Lorna arrived at Detroit with her mother, who, unexpectedly, refused to let her daughter race. The small aft cockpit had to be enlarged so that it would hold a man. The day before the race, however, Lorna's father came, and he announced, "Lorna, you race with Harold."

It was too late to have the aft cockpit made smaller again; Lorna knew that she would have to hold on tight. She didn't realize how tight. The water was exceptionally rough. The combination of hasty carpenter work to redo the cockpit, lightweight

John and Bertha Hacker. The picture was taken at the home of a nephew, evidently at Christmastime, judging from the cards on the wall. *Courtesy Marion Hacker Hurst*

construction, and rough water caused the seat to come apart. She was almost lying down, bumping on the pieces of seat, jamming herself in the cockpit to keep from flying out. Part way into the first heat, as they rounded a corner, the steering jammed and the boat headed at high speed straight for a stone breakwater. As Harold wrestled with the wheel, Lorna realized that one of the pieces of wood that had come loose in her cockpit had jammed the steering gear. She reached back and pulled it out, Harold was able to turn the boat—so close to the breakwater that it almost left varnish there—and off

Miss Wendy, a 21-foot Hackercraft runabout of 1937, powered by a Gray Marine Phantom. Found in storage in Minnesota and restored over seven years, the boat more recently appeared as a period craft in a TV miniseries. *Classic Boating*

they went again. But the delay ended any chance of winning, and they ended up in the pack. In attempting to catch up, however, they made the fastest time of any boat in that heat, 66.087 miles per hour, a new Gold Cup record. In view of this performance, the boating press forecast great things for the craft.

On the way back to the pits the boat seemed sluggish and handled peculiarly. They lifted it out and saw water pouring from all its seams. After it was put back on the trailer, they found considerable water still in the hull, still pouring out. The pounding in the rough water had opened all its seams. It turned out that Hacker had used narrow longitudinal strips for its planking, three-quarters of them 5/8-inch thick. Every fourth plank was of double thickness, a heavier stringer that was to provide the necessary strength to the hull—but did not.

Lorna came out of the boat bruised and stiff from her pounding, and the next day could hardly walk. But she was young and hardy and was well recovered by September 28, when she and Harold were married.

Back at Gravenhurst, the hull was strengthened and the Miller engine, which still was temperamental, further worked over. Next spring everything was put back together, and the boat was taken out and tried. The new construction had changed its balance—at speed, it porpoised badly, finally leaping into the air and diving under. It was fished out, patched up, and tried again, but that was the practical end of *Miss Canada II*. The Wilsons commissioned a *Miss Canada III*—to be designed not by John Hacker, but by Doug Van Patten, although it was said that Van Patten was told to duplicate the fast bottom of the Hacker boat.

Hacker's boats were often lightly built, but usually constructed so that they held together like a basket. Certainly he knew that this boat might race in rough water. We do not know what early conversations took place between him and the elder

Wilson that may have influenced the design, but he seems to have been experimenting with a new idea, to the Wilson's eventual misfortune. Perhaps in some way while changing the cockpit size by last-minute carpentry work, which obviously was slipshod, the whole structure was weakened.

Events might almost have followed a graph of John Hacker's luck during this time. Remember that the Hacker-redesigned *Notre Dame II* came in second in the 1939 President's Cup race? The winner was the Van Patten-designed *Miss Canada III*.

Three-Point Racing Boats

Not many people paid attention to the three-point racing boats when they first developed. Probably Hacker did not, although they would be a growing threat to his creations. Their use began when *Juno*, designed by Adolph Apel and built in his factory at Ventnor, New Jersey, entered the President's Cup race in 1937; although it raced for only one heat, flipping over in the second, it made a new speed record for Gold Cup boats of 84.6 miles per hour. In Miami the following spring it won the event for Gold Cup boats and raised the

record to 89.776. *Juno's* owner took it racing in Europe that summer, so it did not participate in the 1938 Gold Cup race. A homemade entry from California, *Miss Golden Gate,* built as a three-pointer by two young enthusiasts, took part. It lasted the whole course but did not win. But in 1939 a three-point boat, *My Sin,* designed and built by Apel, won easily.

The idea behind the three-pointers was scarcely new; it had been tried in various ways in the past, most recently in a somewhat different form by Hickman with his Sea Sleds. That may be why these revolutionary three-pointers initially attracted so little attention. The first accounts of races in which they ran did not distinguish between them and the traditional hydroplanes.

Three-point boats were so called because at the bow they rested on two sponsons, one on each side, and at the stern on a very small patch of hull. The hull of a three-pointer was concave on the bottom; air rushing between the sponsons lifted the hull so that little weight rested on the water. At speed there was a thin skin of air under each sponson and at the stern the only thing touching

the water was the partly submerged propeller. Craft of this pattern were often called airborne boats. As their speed became better known, some people objected that they were not true boats, but airplanes, and pointed out that working boats of this design would be of little use in open water. But the whole development of hydroplanes had been driven by the desire to lift the hull in order to have as little friction as possible between boats and water. The airborne boats brought this evolution to its logical conclusion.

A Revitalized Hacker Boat Company

In 1935 the Hacker Boat Company received $20,000 from the Reconstruction Finance Corporation, a government body that aided small businesses that had been hit hard by the depression. In the spring of 1937, S. D. McCready announced the appointment of a new sales manager. The new man, C. W. Nugent, had worked for General Motors for 13 years and had also been regional sales manager for "two important boatbuilding concerns." For the Hackercraft company, obviously the economic outlook was improving. Again,

A 1937 51-footer powered by two six-cylinder Scripps, *Bosun* was built by A. L. Beatty of Huron, Ohio, for a Cleveland owner. The only gesture Hacker made toward streamlining in this design was the shape of the mast. *The Mariners' Museum, Newport News, Virginia*

production figures are not available, but Hackercraft's closest competitor was Gar Wood, and Wood's production of runabouts and utilities in 1937 was 260. It may be optimistic to suggest that McCready produced as many Hackercraft that year, but clearly the economic climate was improving.

Hacker continued designing for the company. The Hackercraft catalog issued by the McCready-owned company in 1937 had a picture of *Lockpat II* on the cover and the title page, and a picture of *El Lagarto* on the first page, which said, among other things:

"It is a matter of record that the Hacker Boat Company has contributed more outstanding improvements to the development of fast pleasure craft than, perhaps, the balance of the whole industry at large combined. This Company was among the first to recognize the possibilities of vee-bottom construction and was the producer of the first hydroplane to make 50 miles an hour; the first hydroplane to exceed the 50-mile speed;

the first to build a runabout exceeding 60 miles. Practically every successful hydroplane, as well as every successful conventional type of speed boat, has been largely patterned after innovations first introduced and produced by this organization."

In one sense the statement was correct enough, but the man who had personified all those accomplishments was no longer there. If one substituted the name John L. Hacker for the company name and for the words "this company" and "this organization," the passage would be considerably more accurate.

Of course the small community of boat designers and builders would smile or shake their heads when they saw that paragraph, but the public at large would take it as it was written. There had developed something mean-spirited in Hackercraft advertising that usually kept the company from mentioning Hacker's name. One exception occurred in a much later post–World War II advertisement listing the 30-foot "cabin utility or runabout" that was a long-standing design dating back to 1929. That actually gave John L. Hacker as the designer, but such generosity was rare.

The 1937 catalog listed a 17-foot sport runabout and both a 17-foot and a 19-foot Hackercraft utility, plus 21- and 24-foot cabin utility boats, in all of which "power plants are six-cylinder marine engines." It also offered a new 23-foot Hackercraft, which was essentially the old 22 1/2-footer, with even some of the same descriptive writing in the catalog. The company dropped the old 24-footer. The open boats now had V-shaped windshields; the cabin boats had flat divided windshields with double panes that were hinged at the top and could be opened outward.

There were 26-, 28-, 30-, and 33-foot runabouts. The old 36-foot commuter-cruiser was pictured with the caption "36-foot Hackercraft," and no further description, but the 48-foot commuter still had two pages of pictures and text. A picture of *Lockpat II* illustrated a page on the "Special Department for *Custom*

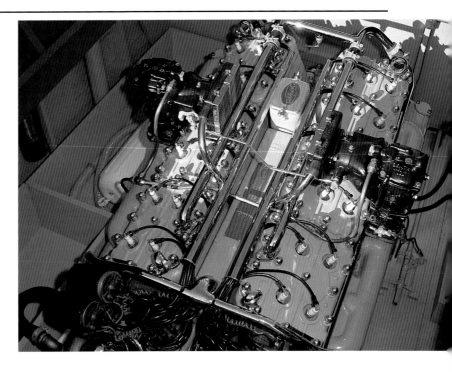

The restored 12-cylinder Scripps engine of *Shooting Star. Classic Boating*

Winner of numerous concourse awards, *Shooting Star* displays its perfect Honduras mahogany against the blue water. *Classic Boating*

A 55-foot cruiser designed by Hacker and launched in 1939. It belonged to a Canadian, Montague Black. *Classic Boating*

Built Designs." Evidently the Special Department had built nothing as striking since that boat was launched. According to the text:

"Despite the fact that such boats are built to special design, the Hackercraft organization is now able to fulfill such custom orders at prices little higher than those of stock models. This is due to the fact that only craftsman labor is employed in our plant. In consequence, these master boatbuilders who are long trained in building the *whole* boat—not merely trained for just one operation—can effect savings of many man hours of work. The years of experience, training and knowledge coupled with a smaller, more efficient organization offer worthwhile economies without sacrifice of fine quality."

It is doubtful that many custom boats were built during that time. But the description of Hacker workers as craftsmen, compared to those of other builders who used mass production—most obviously Chris-Craft—suggests that Hacker's standards of construction were being maintained.

This Hackercraft catalog had no construction information, but present-day restorers have found that the later boats were made as well as the earlier ones. Under Depression constraints, the factory may have used woods that were equally good but less expensive than, for example, the white oak that was the general standard for keels and frames. Toward the back of the catalog was the same page that appeared in earlier books telling about the plant, but this time the headline read, "Hackercraft are built in one of the world's best equipped boat plants . . . by some of America's finest *craftsman* builders." No mention this time of who did the supervising.

In 1938 an announcement in the January issue of *Power Boating* proclaimed that the Hacker

Boat Company was announcing "a complete fleet of highly modernized utility, cabin utility, and runabouts" for that year. A 17-foot utility "should prove extremely popular in view of its moderate price." There was in addition a 19-foot utility that was also available with a cabin.

In the production of utilities, Hackercraft followed the example of Lyman, whose white-painted, lapstrake boats were highly successful during the depression. Chris-Craft, Gar Wood, and others found that utilities now sold at least as well as runabouts. They were open, with only small decks at bow and stern and a narrow strip of decking along each side. The engine was under a box in the middle of the boat. Even when they were built of mahogany, carvel built, and varnished they were less flashy than runabouts, more useful for everyday boating, and had a wider appeal.

"In addition to runabouts in 17-, 19-, 21-, 23-, 26-, and 30-foot lengths, the Hacker Boat Co. has a highly developed 29-foot fast cruiser, which is available in several types," said the *Powerboating* announcement. The picture of the small cruiser showed a tidy boat with a trunk cabin forward and a permanent raised top over the large aft cockpit, the standard arrangement for a cruiser of that size. It was a round-bottom boat, painted white—and it was designed by John L. Hacker, who sold a similar design to Hutchinson, a builder in the Thousand Islands area of the upper St. Lawrence River.

Other John Hacker Designs

John Hacker continued to design V-bottom boats and occasional hydroplanes. The Brooks Boat Company of Saginaw, Michigan, a manufacturer of knock-down boats, in 1937 advertised "*Fleetfoot*— a Hacker-designed V-bottom runabout in 22 1/2- and 24-foot." A photo of *Fleetfoot* showed a compact small runabout flying the Detroit Yacht Club burgee—a boat with only a rear cockpit. According to the text, "This design can be furnished in a 24-foot length and you can build in a cockpit forward and aft of the engine, permitting the operation of the boat and motor from the forward cockpit. To insure proper balance of hull with this arrangement, we provide for installation of the motor further aft." The knock-down kit could be provided with either cyprus or mahogany planking. (The latter of course cost more.) It also could have white oak or mahogany decking, and galvanized iron fittings for fresh water, or copper and brass fittings for salt water.

Even though the boat was a runabout, a build-it-yourself kit did not compete with Hackercraft. There is no evidence that during the existence of the McCready company Hacker designed runabouts or utilities for stock production by anyone else.

Hacker also did jobs for other companies that made unassembled boats. In 1941 he designed a handsome 45-footer for a concern that was well known for its knock-down craft, Bay City Boats. Power in this one could range from a single 125-horsepower engine, which would drive it at 15 miles per hour, to a pair of 200-horsepower

Hacker's ultimate commuter and ultimate streamliner, *Thunderbird*, a 55-footer with two 500-horsepower Kermaths, built by Huskins in Bay City, Michigan, and shipped in 1940 to its owner on Lake Tahoe. A completely streamlined boat, it had its main control station at the front of the cabin in what would be the pilot's position in a passenger aircraft. The open bridge amidships was mainly the way to board, although it had secondary controls used for harbor operation. *The Mariners Museum, Newport News, Virginia*

engines that would increase the speed to 26 miles per hour.

In the several years just before World War II, he designed 58- and 64-foot cruisers for the Fisher Boat Company of Detroit, where the actual builders were the Pouliots, whom Hacker had known when they were building Belle Isle Bear Cats. The boats were semicustom, and Hacker spent some time at the boatyard supervising their construction. An organ was installed in one. One became *Bismillah,* for George Trumbull, and another *Lone Wolf* for Ed Wolfe.

Thunderbird

Some of Hacker's finest work and perhaps the culmination of his commuter designs was *Thunderbird,* for use on Lake Tahoe. In 1939 he received a telegram asking him to come to Palo Alto, California, to discuss the design of a boat; his airfare and expenses would be paid. At that time air travel was still less usual than train travel, and he was delighted at the idea. His family were slightly scared by it, but off he went. In addition to obtaining the commission for the boat he did some sightseeing. His flights went only in the daytime and he had to stop at night; he was not enclosed in a capsule and shot from one end of his journey to the other, as we would be today. He was most impressed by the Grand Canyon and—surprisingly for a man who never went to church—the Mormon temple.

A slim 55-footer with only 12-foot beam, *Thunderbird* had a varnished Honduras mahogany hull and stainless steel deck houses,

Thunderbird,
Hacker's ultimate
commuter with a
streamlined
mahogany hull and
stainless steel
cabin, carries a
group for a short
cruise. *Thunderbird*
can be chartered
by the day.
Classic Boating

and was powered by two 500-horsepower Kermath engines. It was built in 1939 by Huskins in Bay City, Michigan, where Hacker's brother Fred was supervisor. In 1940, *Thunderbird* was shipped by rail to its owner, George Whittell, a real estate magnate whose lakefront estate was named Thunderbird Lodge. Whittell planned to use it for speedy travel around the big lake. Its trial speed before it was shipped to its new owner was over 43 miles per hour. It was double planked throughout and fastened with Monel screws.

Reflecting Whittell's desires, the profile was streamlined like that of an aircraft. The cabin was long and low, the forward end of it a control station separated from the cabin proper by a partition with a door, rather like the pilot's space on a commercial passenger aircraft. Slightly aft of amidships there was an open bridge deck with another set of controls. As the boat was originally designed, this bridge had neither windshield nor top, but both were added by a later owner. In addition to the open bridge, there was a small cockpit near the stern that could seat two or three people. Just forward of it were hatches over a more utilitarian cockpit that gave access to the engines. A telephone connected the pilothouse, the main cabin, and the motor cockpit.

The main cabin had dinettes—furniture resembling restaurant booths—on each side of a central corridor. On each there were two upholstered bench seats facing fore and aft with a table between them; they could be converted to berths, one on each side of the boat. Paneling was mahogany, upholstery was red leather. Aft of the seating space was a galley on one side and a head on the other.

After Whittell's death, *Thunderbird* went to casino owner and car-and-boat collector Bill Harrah, who converted its interior to a "70 mile per hour cocktail lounge," in Joseph Gribbins' words. Carrying 300 gallons of fuel in two tanks, it could circle the lake two times before it needed refueling. While Harrah owned it he had two men wash it down every day and then go over both wood and metal with Pledge furniture polish, using clean Turkish towels. (It remains the largest thing on Lake Tahoe and today can be chartered at a steep fee for cruises on the lake.)

In 1940 Hacker suffered another blow. He lost his St. Clair Shores home. His "dream house, realized, and lost," as his daughter Marion puts it. He and his family moved back to Detroit, where they would live in a series of successively poorer and smaller houses.

At that time, although he did not have another breakdown, Hacker must have been greatly stressed. A family member recalled that at a Friday evening gathering of the extended Hacker family for dinner and cards—about the only social event that Hacker really enjoyed—his wife sent him out to get some napkins. He returned with a package of sanitary napkins.

World War II Approaches

As the depression merged into defense preparations before World War II, many race enthusiasts went into the armed services and the government began to control products that were considered necessary for defense. Building or racing Gold Cup boats became difficult, and commissions to design them became correspondingly rare.

In March 1938 *Yachting* wrote, "According to rumors, George Reis will be very much on the job

this year with a new boat, designed by Hacker and equipped with the Reis-Menasco engine built for but not used in *El Lagarto.*" It would be interesting to know if a move was actually made in that direction, and perhaps abandoned because of the growing restrictions. Time passed and Reis never raced again. He spent his summers at Bolton's Landing, using *El Lagarto* as a speedy runabout on Lake George.

The last Gold Cup race before the war was in 1941. The Montauk Yacht Club, whose boat had won the previous year, felt that it did not have the money to stage the race properly. The irrepressible Horace Dodge Jr., owner of several race boats and heir to the Dodge millions, volunteered his home

base of Detroit. When the Detroit Yacht Club demurred, he said he would underwrite the race. That was enough to start the publicity drums beating for Detroit.

The Detroit Yacht Club sent invitations to 18 possible entrants—and received three answers. One was from a man who had sold his boat, one from an owner who said that he had no crew, and one from an owner who said that his boat needed parts that the government would not release. So Detroit, being discreet, simply announced that the defense load was too great for it to hold the race.

Whereupon Dodge, still pushing, managed to convince the Red Bank, New Jersey, Yacht Club

to stage the 1941 Gold Cup race. But Dodge did not enter any of his own craft and only one contestant showed up. Disgusted, that owner was about to go home, but the officials persuaded him to let his boat cruise easily around the course and be declared the winner.

World War II

The Hacker Boat Company did defense work during World War II. The company built 45-foot picket boats for the navy, to a standard design that originated elsewhere. The boats had twin engines, and both propellers were right-handed screws instead of being opposed, an intentional feature— it let engines be replaced or interchanged

A 64-foot Hacker cruiser built by Fisher in 1939, *Lone Wolf* was owned by Ed Wolfe, who ranged the East Coast with it. © *Mystic Seaport, Rosenfeld Collection, Mystic, Connecticut*

without regard to the way the propellers turned. But as a result, the users found that they couldn't dock the boats starboard-side-to without the help of a tug.

In early 1944 the company won an "Army-Navy E," a reward for the excellence of its war production. That permitted it to fly a special flag and each employee to wear a special lapel badge. "John Tesmer, superintendent of the Hacker plant for 25 years, and associated with the founder, Naval Architect John Hacker, for years before that time, will accept the badges for the men, to whom the badges will be issued following the official ceremonies."

The picket boats were built a long way from their destination and then ferried to the Norfolk Navy Yard, under navy contract, by Capt. Jay Ottinger. In convoys of two or three at a time they went down the Clinton River to Lake St. Clair, through the Detroit River and Lake Erie to Buffalo and Tonawanda, then via the Erie Canal to Troy, where they transferred to the Hudson River, then went into the Atlantic to

Cape May, then through canals to the Chesapeake and on to Norfolk. The total run was about 1,250 miles.

Hacker, whom the Japanese Navy had approached to design a PT boat before World War I, was largely ignored by the U.S. Navy during World War II. One unlikely explanation says that his German family background made him suspect. Another says that he was ignored because he was not attached to a large plant that could mass-produce wartime boats. His reputation had dimmed. He may just have been overlooked because of fortune's roll of the dice, drastic wartime reorganization often missing available talent.

Hacker's life during this time was further diminished as his two daughters married and his son was drafted. At home now in a small house there was only his wife, with whom he was not entirely compatible.

For the war he designed nothing major. His best-known wartime products were 34-foot radio-controlled target tow boats, of Hacker runabout

designs, that were built by his old company. They were equipped with 550-horsepower V-12 Kermath engines, and had radio controls built into their front cockpits. It was said that initially they were intended to carry bombs and to ram enemy ships. If that was correct, it proved impractical—the most obvious objection being that the Germans could jam the radio signals that controlled the boats—but they did well towing targets for gunnery practice.

Before arranging for construction of these boats, the navy tried out samples from all three of the best-known builders. The inspector reported, "After about a half-hour the Chris-Craft shipped a sea and was suffering from excessive pounding and was tied up at her berth." Further on he said, "It is noteworthy that although Hacker was heavier by 1,700 pounds than Gar Wood, power consumption was less at all speeds above 35 horsepower." And further still, "The Hacker was about 25 percent softer riding, due to its reduced pounding force, than the Gar Wood." (The reduced pounding, of

course, was due to the convex bottom.) After looking at both the Wood and the Hacker plants, he noted that "The Hacker plant is smaller but laid out with equal efficiency." The report also included the information that the Hacker Boat Company had shipped 10 of these models to the French government in 1937. They were not new designs.

When they first came from the factory and were taken to Lake St. Clair to be tested, the target-towing boats were painted yellow, so that they could be seen easily as they went through their remote-controlled maneuvers. On duty, they were painted gray with black numbers on their bows. After the war, when they became surplus, some of them were bought by clever purchasers and changed back to Hacker runabouts.

During the war Hacker became chief designer for the Eddy Marine Corporation, which had him improve the bottom design of an air-sea rescue boat and do other nautical-design odd jobs as the war continued.

Hacker's major contribution during World War II was to redesign the U.S. Army Air Force crash rescue boat. Here is his new version, in June 1944. *The Mariners' Museum, Newport News, Virginia*

Head-on, *Pardon ME* **shows its art deco bow design.** *Classic Boating*

Chapter Six

MILESTONE BOATS
Hacker's Later Designs

In the spring of 1946 Nelson Zimmer, a young naval architect just back from World War II, stopped in to see John Hacker. Hacker's office at that time was above an auto showroom on Jefferson Avenue in Detroit. Zimmer had known him before the war when sizable pleasure cruisers of Hacker's design were built at the Fisher Boat Company, where Zimmer then worked.

In the course of their discussion, Hacker asked what Zimmer planned to do, and the younger man said that he supposed he would reestablish himself somewhere as a boat designer. Hacker said that he had a spare drafting room, and would Zimmer like to use it? Zimmer asked about the rent, but Hacker said that he wouldn't charge anything. Zimmer gratefully accepted the offer.

Hacker's offices consisted of a reception area, two drafting rooms with a connecting door, and a storage room. There was never a receptionist or secretary in the reception room; Hacker did all his own typing. He worked in one of the drafting rooms, Zimmer moved into the other.

Before joining the navy, Zimmer had worked early in the war at a shipyard in Toledo, Ohio, not far from Detroit. He owned a 16-cylinder Cadillac, which he had purchased used during the depression, when such cars were cheap. When he went off to war, he left his car in storage at Toledo. After returning to Detroit and accepting Hacker's offer of free office space, he went to collect his imposing car and found that over the years in storage, its tires had rotted. Tires for that car were large and expensive, and navy service had not left Zimmer with a great deal of money. Hacker bought a new set of tires for him.

Zimmer stayed in Hacker's spare office for three years, doing his own work. He did not work on Hacker's designs, and eventually he went off to develop a fiberglass boat company.

Zimmer recalls that Hacker was disappointed that his son, following World War II service and discharge as a first sergeant in the Army Air Force, had taken a civilian job working in the Air Logistic Command at Dayton, Ohio, rather than returning and becoming a partner in his father's design office. The elder Hacker may for a time have looked on the youthful Zimmer as a substitute son.

His real son, John A. Hacker, became a career Air Force civilian. Initially he was located at Dayton as supervisor of a group of marine equipment technicians, who supported a fleet of rescue boats that the Air Force operated. In 1951 or 1952 he and his technicians moved to Mobile, Alabama, and in 1962 he went to Sacramento, California. Somewhere along the way, he moved from boats to more general administration. Once or twice a year he visited Detroit. It was just as well that he had a separate job; from time to time he made loans to his father.

While Zimmer was sharing the office, John L. Hacker usually worked late into the evening; he was bored with his wife and found things dull at home. It was the classic problem of a self-made man: over the years he had gained wider interests and understandings while she, by the customs of the day, had remained at home with little opportunity to expand her interests. Hacker was not a particularly sociable man. Although he belonged to the Detroit Yacht Club, he seldom went there except to have a swim, to watch races, or to engage in other activities that interested him professionally. His greatest social pleasure was in gatherings of his own large Hacker clan.

There is no indication that Hacker ever thought of himself as a genius, although in his last years he pointed out with reasonable humility that he had designed more boats than any other naval architect. But geniuses often have eccentricities, and he had several. There were the ones that clustered about his physical culture enthusiasms. Little wonder that he and his wife were somewhat at odds; these days he often ate alone. Mrs. Hacker was reputed to be a good cook, but he wanted what he considered healthful meals, which could only leave her frustrated.

John L. Hacker at his drawing board. *The Mariners' Museum, Newport News, Virginia*

He continued to do designs for his former company—an indication, Zimmer thought, that he had some business ability and was sufficiently astute to take the fees rather than let his emotions intrude.

Those who knew him then have said that he always seemed tense and nervous, and they usually attributed that to his history of breakdowns. He was not a patient man. He worked hard and always seemed to work fast; often he produced the overall design of his boats but left out the details, saying that any competent boatbuilder would know what they should be. He knew, having been a boatbuilder himself. One result of his speedy work was that he did not number or date his designs, something that has caused problems for present-day archivists. Other archival problems arise because he would sometimes cannibalize an old design, taking parts of it to use for a new boat. (Other designers also did this—but they kept better records.)

At that time, he was a vegetarian who brought fruit and health food to the office for his lunch. He took a week or two each year to go off to a sanitarium run by Bernarr MacFadden, a physical culture guru of the time. He also usually went on midwinter vacations to a "rest ranch" in Florida where he would fast for several days, taking only water, and then build himself up again on a vegetarian diet.

He was a reserved man, but behind his facade he was gentle and generous to people whom he liked, as Nelson Zimmer found. Although he never went to church he did not swear, smoke, or drink, and he was offended by others whose behavior overstepped the normal bounds. Sometimes people who did not know him found him crusty. Capt. Jay Ottinger describes John L. as "a tall, dignified, balding gentleman, very dedicated but not stubborn when an owner or builder wanted changes." Possibly one reason for his normal lack of stubbornness was that his clients usually had great respect for his ideas. It was known that if someone wanted a boat that he considered wrong, he simply

would refuse to design it. On one occasion he told a General Motors executive politely that he had to go elsewhere and find another designer to do what he asked. The man eventually came back and accepted Hacker's guidance.

The Largest Runabout

Perhaps Hacker should have been more stubborn with one client, Charles P. Lyon, who commissioned him to design an unusual boat, who no doubt discussed the design with him at some length beforehand, and who wanted something that was scarcely practicable. The boat was to be built by the Hutchinson Boat Works at Alexandria Bay, New York, on the upper St. Lawrence, near Lyon's summer home; Lyon, evidently in a hurry to get the job done, wanted construction to start before the design was finished. Hacker probably demurred but could not change his client's determination.

Hacker had previously designed commuter-runabouts for Lyon that were built by boatyards

on the upper St. Lawrence. The new boat was to be a super runabout and was reminiscent of such former Hacker boats as *Lockpat II.* The Hutchinson Boat Works built it at Alexandria Bay in 1947 and 1948. It was 48 feet long, 11 feet in beam, and had a 3-foot draft. The bottom was double-planked mahogany on oak frames, and the sides were double: fore-and-aft planking on the outside, diagonal planking on the inside. It had a forward cuddy cabin, unlike more normally sized runabouts. A 1,500-horsepower Packard V-12 engine drove it.

According to the owner's wishes, construction on the boat was started before the design was finished. It is hard to imagine a better recipe for confusion. As Hacker completed parts of the boat he fed the blueprints to the builder, but sometimes the parts did not seem quite to fit together and sometimes he changed them as he went along. Hutchinson, understandably irritated by this procedure, sometimes did things its own

Alberta, a Hacker-designed 44-footer built by the Fisher Boat Works of Detroit in 1946. It was powered by two six-cylinder Hall-Scotts. *The Mariners' Museum, Newport News, Virginia*

way and sometimes neglected to make the changes that Hacker sent.

The completed boat was named *Pardon Me.* There is speculation as to the choice of name. Though from a little distance it looks like a typical runabout, thanks to Hacker's eye for proportion, actually it is huge. Was the name an apology for the space the boat took up in narrow channels and restricted harbors, or perhaps for the conspicuous consumption that it represented?

Pardon Me required a two-man crew, not unusual for a boat almost 50 feet long. One man steered; the other operated a gear lever placed amidships. In its first season's trials it had problems. The rudder and the hydraulic steering gear were erratic and the boat was hard to steer—sometimes frighteningly so. The power of the engine, unless it was carefully handled, bent the propeller out of pitch.

Lyon, who was ill and spent only parts of that summer with it, was not interested in the adjustments and tuning often needed for a new custom-built boat. At the end of the season it went back to Hutchinson and was put up for sale, supposedly for $50,000. It sat there for three years until the price came down to a reported $12,000, paid by Dick Locke, the Detroit resident who had owned the Hacker-designed-and-built *Lockpat II.* He moved *Pardon Me* to Detroit and renamed it *Lockpat III.* After Locke died, the boat went through several owners, one of whom gave it a thorough restoration. Finally, it was presented to the Antique Boat Museum at Clayton, New York, where it now resides.

A more recent assessment of its steering problem brought out that Hacker provided a change in the shape of its bottom to Hutchinson during the time when the drawings were flowing piecemeal from designer to builder, but Hutchinson

never made it. No doubt that part of the boat had already been built. Under the peculiar circumstances surrounding the design and construction, it is hard to blame the builder. The museum has given the necessary thought to the problem and apparently has been able to fix it, and *Pardon Me* again runs in upper St. Lawrence waters.

Designs of the 1940s

During these years Hacker continued to design boats for the Canadian builders on the Muskoka Lakes. The reason he was permitted this deviation from his agreement with the McCreadys is unknown. Perhaps he paid the Hacker Boat Company a percentage of his fees. Perhaps so few boats were built from any one plan that they were considered custom designs. In 1950 he produced for Greavette the drawings for 17- and 31-foot boats with inboard-outboard propulsion. In 1952 he did a 20-foot V-bottom design for Duke.

The boats had single cockpits fore and aft of the engine. Duke built two, then stretched the design to 22 feet, which permitted him to fit in a double forward cockpit.

Despite his reputation as a designer of smaller craft, Hacker was particularly interested in cruisers, and turned out many of them. One 36-foot sport cruiser design appeared in *The Rudder* for March 1945. There were aspects of a runabout in it—in the downward curve of the sheer near the bow, in its driver's seat in an open cockpit behind a windshield, and perhaps in the minimal accommodations under a small trunk cabin. There were two berths, a tiny galley on a shelf, and a crowded toilet shielded only by a curtain, all tightly fitted in.

A 42-footer for use at New Orleans and on the Gulf of Mexico was quite a different proposition. Its design appeared in February of 1949. It had two much less crowded berths, a full galley,

Pardon Me, **48 feet in length, 11 feet in beam, and drawing 3 feet. Hacker–designed, it was launched in 1948 by Hutchinson on the upper St. Lawrence River. It can be seen today at the Antique Boat Museum, Clayton, New York.** *Classic Boating*

Moving away at speed, *Pardon Me* could be a runabout of normal length unless one looks carefully at the size of its passengers. *Classic Boating*

and a full toilet room. They were under a forward cabin and were arranged somewhat like the accommodations of the 36-footer, though with much more room. Then amidships was a raised "main cabin"—a combined wheelhouse and living room, which had a folding berth on either side. The twin Chrysler Royal engines that drove it at 24 miles per hour were under hatches in the deck at the stern, working through V-drives. Even at this date, the magazine thought it interesting to report that the boat had an electric lighting plant and electric refrigerator.

Hacker also worked with the Kehrig Manufacturing Company, which produced what were known as Kehrig-Hackerform standard 32-foot steel cruisers, a notable departure from his usual wooden boats.

Hacker Boat Company, 1946–1954

A postwar catalog for Hackercraft—produced by McCready's Hacker Boat Company—listed 19-, 22-, 26-, and 30-foot utilities and runabouts. They all had V-shaped windshields. In describing the 30-footers, it gave unusual credit: "No other

builder offers a stock model with a convex bottom which eliminates 98 percent of the pounding in rough water. This is a development of John L. Hacker and the Hacker Boat Co. dating back to 1929." The 26-footers also had the convex bottoms that Hacker gradually built into his larger craft. The smaller ones remained concave-bottomed.

As early as 1928 Hacker had begun to use bottoms of cedar. The 26-footers in this catalog are described as having mahogany planking on sides and deck, and double bottoms of Port Orford cedar. The description of the 30-footers' construction is less specific, but they almost certainly had cedar bottoms as well. In another rare departure from the company custom of omitting the designer's name, this catalog said, "The Hacker custom built department is in an excellent position to build your new boat to the design of your naval architect, or to the design of John L. Hacker."

In 1949 the McCready company brought out the Hackercraft Express Cruiser, a 28-foot, 6-inch boat with 9-foot, 4-inch beam, similar to Hacker's 36-footer design in *The Rudder* for 1945. The two designs showed his growing

interest in pocket-size cruisers, a type that he helped develop.

The Hackercraft boat had a small trunk cabin forward, followed by a raised bridge behind a windshield, and a small aft cockpit. A pocket edition of fast cruisers that Hacker had designed in the past, it was too small to permit a forward cockpit or to provide more than three berths. Its hull was planked with Port Orford cedar and was painted white. It had the convex V-bottom. Its top speed was 34 miles per hour.

The boat was first advertised in early 1949 and met with sufficient enthusiasm that it became the front cover boat for the January 1950 annual boat show issue of *Motor Boat* magazine. None of the Hackercraft advertisements had mentioned the designer. The cover note inside the magazine, however, said:

"This month we have a boat designed by John L. Hacker which, with two big Chryslers, is really just about the hottest thing in the way of speed that anyone could ask for. Furthermore, it has full cruising accommodations with berths, galley, lavatory, etc. A real cruising boat with the speed of a fast runabout.

"This small beauty was one of the first of a type of fast compact cruiser that has become increasingly popular up to the present day."

An advertisement on the inside of that same issue offered the new 1950 Hackercraft 22-foot Sport Dolphin. Across the page ran the line, "America's Finest Craft—Created by America's Foremost Designer!" It was a line that it used in other ads, always without naming the designer in question; although it would seldom use Hacker's name, this at least came close. Most readers would assume that John Hacker was the person who was meant as designer of a Hacker Company boat.

This particular model was designed by Hacker, but it was scarcely a fair example of his work. It was designed down to the level of lowest possible cost. It had a front cockpit, but that was separated from the rest of the boat only by a narrow deck behind the single bench seat. Behind this narrow cross deck was an open space with an engine under a box in the middle of it. The boat was more a utility than the runabout suggested by the Dolphin name. Flat sided, white painted, it could have been made of plywood, although it was not. It might be a useful working craft, but it was not an attractive pleasure boat. There has been a theory that its unpopularity caused the eventual demise of the company—but that did not come for another seven years. The Sport Dolphin had very little to do with it.

The boat may, however, have been a symptom that the company was not in the best financial health. It made only 8 or 10 boats per month at this time and employed 16 people, including those in the office. The Korean War

The post–World War II 19-foot Hackercraft utility was essentially a duplicate of the depression-era 19-footer designed by Hacker for the McCready-owned Hacker Boat Company. Smaller boats and utility designs grew popular after World War II. The more generally useful utilities in time largely replaced runabouts. *From a Hacker Boat Company Catalog*

This 30-foot sedan—an enclosed utility—offered in 1948 by the McCreadys' Hacker Boat Company had a top speed of 46 miles per hour with a Scripps V-12. It was based on an older John Hacker design. *The Mariners' Museum, Newport News, Virginia*

began in 1950. Other builders, such as Chris-Craft, had had enough of government red tape during World War II and this time avoided government contracts. But in 1952, according to the Mount Clemens *Daily Monitor* of January 22:

" The Hacker Boat Company, long-established Mount Clemens manufacturers of custom-built marine craft, today was awarded a government contract to build 25 ocean-going picket boats for the navy.

"S. Dudley McCready, owner of the firm and a boat designer for 30 years, will also direct the preparation of detailed plans for 123 other picket boats for five other firms with contracts."

The company surely welcomed this further source of income.

While turning out navy boats, the McCreadys also continued to produce some pleasure boats. In the January 1953 *Motor Boating* they advertised:

"Hackercraft. Sleek, powerful, polished mahogany runabouts like this will be available only

in limited quantity in 1953, but Hacker Boat Company is prepared to take a limited number of orders up to the point where such work will not interfere with present navy orders."

The company offered 26- and 30-footers, both runabouts and utilities with or without sedan tops. During this period the pleasure boat designs had continued to improve. A Hacker historian, Tom Flood, has owned and restored a number of Hackercraft and has found that the long-popular 26-foot model in its 1950 version is the best-handling and best-riding boat of them all.

It was just as well that Hackercraft continued building a few pleasure boats, for after it built some 30 naval craft, near the end of the Korean War the navy canceled the contract, leaving the builders with the materials bought and on hand for producing another 20 boats. Whatever settlement the government made came slowly. It was said that Mrs. McCready put some of her family money into the company to steady it.

On May 28, 1954, the *Daily Monitor* published an announcement by "Sam McCready, Hacker sales manager" (S. Dudley Jr.) that the company was producing "a sturdy new type of outboard boat" that a 25-horsepower motor could push to 26 miles per hour. Stem, keel, and "apron" were white oak. Planking was made of marine plywood. Trim was mahogany. The news story told how quickly these boats could be built—"with almost assembly line speed"—even though they adhered to the best building practices. The company was apparently looking for a speedy way of getting back into the public market and supporting itself again, and perhaps was employing the plywood in order to use up some of the material left on its hands after the loss of the navy contract.

About 1954 John Tesmer, the longtime superintendent of the Hackercraft factory, retired. Russ Pouliot, an experienced boatbuilder who had worked several times with John Hacker over the years, became superintendent for the company.

Soon the 26-foot Hackercraft three-cockpit runabout was the largest boat the company advertised. It had a convex bottom made of double-planked Port Orford Cedar, with mahogany sides and deck. The forward deck had a moderately high crown, which probably required the V-shaped windshield. Depending on the engine installed, it could run at up to 48 miles per hour. The Hacker Boat Company was one of the few manufacturers who still offered such a boat, and it was obviously a John Hacker design.

Gold Cup Boats, 1947–1957

In 1947 Hacker designed the Gold Cup racing boat *My Sweetie* for two Detroit men, Ed Gregory and Ed Schoenherr (this Ed Gregory was the son of the Belle Isle Gregory who introduced the Bear Cats). It was a 30-footer powered by a 1,710-cubic-inch Allison engine.

The old Hacker Boat Company was no longer interested in custom racing boats, so this

The Hacker Boat Company continued to build three-cockpit runabouts after most other builders stopped, although the boats may have been standard models built only to order. Now they usually had convex bottoms of cedar, although the sides and deck were mahogany. This 1948 22-footer is a Hacker design. *The Mariners' Museum, Newport News, Virginia*

Sirocco, a post–World War II Hacker cruiser, has the typical Hacker hull with tumble home at the stern and flare at the bow. *The Mariners' Museum, Newport News, Virginia*

one was built in Bay City, Michigan, by Les Staudacher, a builder whom Hacker had previously employed to produce some cruisers in the 36- to 52-foot range. The commission for *My Sweetie* began Staudacher's notable career as a builder of racing boats. Staudacher recalled: "John came up and helped us lay it out on the floor, because all we had, was just a set of lines and we had to develop everything full size. We worked that out together. We traded ideas, both construction and design."

My Sweetie's first season, 1948, was devoted to getting it in proper tune. In the Gold Cup race at Detroit it had an accident—for reasons that were given differently in each report—that put a hole in its bottom. Its driver, known as Wild Bill Cantrell, slammed it onto the nearest shore to keep it from sinking.

It was entered in the Silver Cup race, a Detroit contest, in which it was said to bounce

dangerously. "Cantrell was forced to cut *Sweetie's* speed before the leaping beat it to pieces."

That fall in the President's Cup race in Washington, it had a burst of speed that made it the leader in the first heat, but it was unable to come out for either of the remaining heats. *Motor Boating* commented that "It is going to be the boat to beat when all the kinks are worked out of its hull and power plant." But the kinks were still there.

Hacker went back to his drawing board and reworked the bottom of the boat. By the 1949 season, it was behaving differently. A newspaper report on the Gold Cup race dated July 2 said:

"A Louisville business man, Wild Bill Cantrell, who'd rather risk his neck driving fast boats and fast autos than eat, demonstrated this afternoon on a sunny and smooth Detroit River before 200,000 spectators that the best speed boat combination in America is the red and shiny *My*

Sweetie with him crouched in the single cockpit behind its steering wheel."

In the first heat the accelerator pedal suddenly failed. Cantrell reached into the engine space, took hold of the fuel control rod and finished the heat with one hand on the rod and one on the wheel. He managed to finish third. Then in each of the following two heats he led the next boat by a quarter-mile.

A 1949 *Motor Boating* piece called it "a sweet-running hydroplane designed by John Hacker," and commented on its ability to turn nimbly and its level ride. These were probably made possible by its propeller, which was nearly amidships—a far cry from the early Hacker propellers that were placed a foot or more behind the hull—and the bronze skeg that completely enclosed the propeller shaft, further reducing turbulence. "Gar Wood has suggested that this boat will start a new trend in propeller placement."

In 1949 the Buffalo Launch Club held its first regatta in 15 years. In the race for unlimited boats "the smooth riding *My Sweetie* literally ran away from the field." In the report on the race, Horace Dodge was named as owner of the boat.

Finally that year, according to *Motor Boating* for November, "*My Sweetie,* Horace Dodge's superb combination of Hacker Hull and Allison engine, with Bill Cantrell doing the steering, scored another walkaway victory in the featured event of the President's Cup Regatta at Washington, D.C."

The reason for the transfer of ownership to Dodge after the Gold Cup race is unclear. Perhaps its original owners found that maintaining a racing boat was more expensive than they had supposed. Perhaps Dodge offered them a price they could not refuse.

At this time the three-point racers were beginning to appear in some strength. They were at first treated with kindly condescension by other

My Sweetie, Hacker's winning Gold Cup boat of 1949, a 30-footer powered by a 1,710-ci Allison engine. © Mystic Seaport, Rosenfeld Collection, Mystic, Connecticut

My Sweetie at speed, with Hacker's autograph.
Courtesy Marion Hacker Hurst

racers, until it suddenly became obvious that they were dangerously fast competitors. In the 1950 Gold Cup, *My Sweetie* faced a three-point boat from Seattle, *Slo-Mo-Shun IV* and another three-pointer from the East, Guy Lombardo's *Tempo VI* as well as a mixed fleet of other three-pointers and conventional hydroplanes.

Bill Cantrell ran *My Sweetie* in the qualification runs, then took out another Dodge boat to see how it was behaving. It turned over, severely bruising Cantrell. He gamely drove *My Sweetie,* however, for the first heat of the race. The two leaders turned out to be *Sweetie* and *Slo-Mo,* who battled for first place—but *Slo-Mo* eventually lapped *Sweetie* a few feet short of the finish.

Cantrell was in considerable pain from his injuries, so Lou Fageol, another experienced driver, took over. *Sweetie, Slo-Mo,* and *Tempo* were the only competitors left; the others had dropped out. *My Sweetie* was having engine trouble and had to be towed out onto the course, but Fageol and a platoon of mechanics labored over it, and three minutes before the starting gun, the engine came to life.

The race began. *Sweetie* took and held the lead. It traveled so fast that its oil cooler scoop was not picking up enough water. Fageol tried to nurse it along, but it halted a little way short of the finish line. *Slo-Mo-Shun* zoomed past to win the heat; *Tempo* came along to be second. *Sweetie* did not finish the second heat and was not entered in the third.

Hacker was an innovator, but he did not like the three-pointers. The April 1951 *Motor Boating* published two articles side by side. John Hacker wrote one in favor of the conventional hydroplane. He pointed out that the airborne boats could only be used on smooth waters and that they did not have much practical value. He used his own latest designs to show what conventional hydroplanes could do.

The other article, praising the multipoint hydroplane, was by Ted Jones, who had designed some of those boats. He pointed out that they used much less fuel and needed much less power to attain their speeds. They accelerated more quickly; their great width, taking their sponsons into account, made them less likely to upset on a

turn; they rode more easily than even a conventional runabout.

The three-pointers may have been more like airplanes than like boats, they may not have had much practical value as sea-going vessels, but as racers they would not be stopped. Hacker's *My Sweetie* and another of his racers yet to come would fight the rear guard action against the airborne boats.

At the 1950 President's Cup race, *My Sweetie* came in third. When the racing season was over, Dodge had its sides raised to make it stiffer and its fuel tanks moved to improve its balance, or so he thought. In the 1951 Gold Cup race in Seattle it finished sixth.

Miss Pepsi

Hacker unveiled a new racing boat in 1950. It had two Allison 1,710-ci engines mounted fore and aft so that the drive ends faced each other; the power produced by each one went into a gearbox that carried it to a single propeller shaft. It was a complicated arrangement, but one that Gar Wood had used in his multi-engine racing boats of the past. It was not a three-pointer but a conventional hydroplane; its hull was described as having "twin vee steps."

This boat, *Miss Pepsi,* was built for the Dossin brothers of Detroit, who had owned a former *Miss Pepsi.* The new boat was thus a second one with the same name, but no numeral II was added—a

Out of the water, *My Sweetie* shows its slim hull form, its double rudders, and the revolutionary propeller location with its streamlined skeg. © *Mystic Seaport, Rosenfeld Collection, Mystic, Connecticut*

cause of some confusion. That fall, driven by Chuck Thompson who would handle it most of its life, it won all three heats at the President's Cup races. Coming in second, but well behind, was *My Sweetie*, and others trailed along farther back.

Next year it went to the Gold Cup race in Seattle, where it was a challenger against the champion Seattle three-pointer, *Slo-Mo-Shun V.* In its first heat on its fifth circuit of the course, it stopped dead and did not finish. It started in the second heat, but its engine died at the first turn from what *Yachting* called "its oil-losing trouble." *Slo-Mo-Shun V* won. *Hornet*, owned by Horace Dodge, designed and driven by Wild Bill Cantrell, the former driver of *My Sweetie*, came in second.

Back in the East, at the President's Cup race, the Hacker boat again won all three heats. "Thompson demonstrated that *Miss Pepsi* is the top flight Gold Cup boat—east of the Rockies, of course," commented *Motor Boating*. Only two other boats had twice won the President's Cup,

George Reis' *El Lagarto* and Clell Perry's *Notre Dame*, both before World War II.

So in 1952, back to Seattle went Thompson and *Miss Pepsi*. The two boats that it needed to beat were *Slo-Mo-Shun IV* and *Slo-Mo-Shun V*, both Seattle-built three-pointers.

The three boats hit the starting line together. The field fell in behind. *Slo-Mo V* took the lead, *Pepsi* about 100 yards behind. In maneuvering at the turns, *Miss Pepsi* found herself on the receiving end of the rooster tail—the great flow of water thrown into the air by the half-submerged propellers of three-pointers—from *Slo-Mo V*, which at one point bashed in its engine cowling.

The other Seattle boat, *Slo-Mo-Shun IV*, at the end of its fourth lap threw its propeller. Its engine suddenly raced and had to be turned off. It was towed from the course.

The duel between *Miss Pepsi* and *Slo-Mo-Shun V* continued, *Pepsi* following at the heels of the other boat. At the first turn on their sixth lap

Slo-Mo V suddenly slowed and stopped. It had been pushed so hard that its cylinder block had overheated and cracked. *Pepsi,* traveling at 103.972 miles per hour, whizzed by and went on to win the heat.

Before the next heat, the owner of *Slo-Mo-Shun IV* transferred the propeller of *Slo-Mo V* to it, and it was again in the race.

Two of the other boats had dropped out of the race, so the second heat consisted of *Miss Pepsi, Slo-Mo-Shun IV,* and *Such Crust IV,* driven by Cantrell. Just after the heat began *Such Crust IV* exploded, sending pieces of boat in all directions and bursting into flames. Cantrell went overboard, was quickly fished out by a rescue boat, and was sent to the nearest hospital to treat his second and third degree burns. (He recovered and in due course was racing again.)

Meanwhile *Pepsi* and *Slo-Mo IV* were racing down the backstretch unaware of the accident and the red rockets that a Coast Guard boat sent up.

At the second turn Pepsi's complicated gearbox came apart and it ground to a halt. The driver of *Slo-Mo-Shun IV,* Stanley Dollar, arriving back at the judges' barge as the Coast Guard was shooting up more rockets, steered over to the barge to ask if the race was canceled. By then the Coast Guard had subdued the flames and pulled the wreckage out of the way, so the officials told him to go on alone and finish the heat.

The final heat was run by *Slo-Mo-Shun IV* and one other boat that dropped out at the end of the third lap. *Slo-Mo-Shun IV* won the Gold Cup. *Miss Pepsi* was second on points.

On September 20 and 21, 1952, Chuck Thompson drove *Miss Pepsi* to its third victory in the President's Cup race. It beat four three-point boats. Wrote *Yachting:*

"The annual Washington regatta during those years has attracted unlimited fleets, second only to those that appeared for Gold Cup contests. . . not one of the challengers has been able to give the big

Miss Pepsi, Hacker's ultimate champion multistep racer of 1950. It was the last of the traditional planing race boats in the Unlimited Class. This is the 1956 President's Cup race. *Courtesy Dossin Great Lakes Museum, Detroit*

In 1963 *Miss Pepsi's* driver, Chuck Thompson, and Miss Michigan ride the boat into the space built for it in the Dossin Great Lakes Museum at Detroit, as city officials and members of the Dossin family look on. The Dossins, owners of *Miss Pepsi*, built the museum. *Courtesy Dossin Great Lakes Museum, Detroit*

twin-Allison powered conventional hydro a semblance of a race. Designed by Hacker and built by Staudacher, the Dossin craft has held lap, heat, and race records for the Washington course."

But then the boat was retired for several years, and when it came back in 1955 it no longer distinguished herself, even though it was driven again by Thompson. It gained some notoriety, however, in the Gold Cup race of 1956 at Detroit—a race in which sportsmanship was redefined.

The initial winner, *Thriftway*, from Seattle, was disqualified because it had hit the number 27 marker during its seventh lap. *Miss Pepsi* had come in second and on this decision stepped up to first. The owner of *Thriftway* filed a protest with the Inboard Racing Commission. Within 24 hours five other protests were filed. Horace Dodge, typically going off in a different direction, added to the

confusion by obtaining a "show cause" order from a local court to have the race declared "no contest" because of a difference he had had with the officials over the qualifying runs before the race.

In the climate that followed all this, the owners of unlimited racers set up their own racing commission, although they did place it under the overall authority of the American Power Boat Association. In time Horace Dodge was pacified and the Inboard Racing Commission gave the cup back to *Thriftway*. *Miss Pepsi* was again declared second—not a bad showing for a six-year-old boat. (Today it can still be seen in the Dossin Great Lakes Museum at Detroit.)

In 1956 or 1957 Hacker designed two more racers for Dodge. They were to be bigger and better versions of *Miss Pepsi*. But Dodge's mother controlled the family fortune. She was unhappy over one of his impending divorces, and she cut

off the money. He was also becoming an alcoholic, and his health and energy were fading. The boats were never built. Thompson continued to race; in 1966, in the Gold Cup race at Detroit, he was driving the three-pointer *Smirnoff* when it hit a swell at high speed and disintegrated. He was killed.

Air-Sea Rescue Boat, 1952

Hacker's *Oregon Kid,* of 1913, was considered the first true hydroplane racer. Now in the 1940s and 1950s Hacker had brought the form to its highest level, designing the ultimate conventional hydroplane racers. These boats could go faster than many of the three-point racers that now were becoming the favorites. But the speed potential for the three-pointers, as long as they operated in smooth water, was too great. They soon took over racing. In open water, however, three-point boats were practically useless; when seaworthiness was needed, the conventional hydroplane form still provided the fastest boats.

An example of such a vessel was a 94-foot Air Force rescue boat of Hacker's design that was completed at the Detroit Basin in 1952. Officially it was said to be a Huron-Eddy design, but the drawings were all made in Hacker's office. Huron-Eddy gave some technical support, but essentially Hacker did the work. Major features of the boat were the Hacker-Fairline propulsion units developed from *My Sweetie* and *Miss Pepsi.* They allowed this boat's three Packard engines to be lifted out through deck hatches, complete with shafts and propellers.

Phil Bolger, who worked about a year for Hacker in 1951 when he was designing this boat and others, has said that "he was very good to work for, gentle in his corrections and not very secretive. He was a physical culturist and would demonstrate in the office that he could do 40 push-ups without breathing hard." Bolger added that although he was a scholar of classical music, Hacker seemed to be more interested in its technical details and history than in listening to it.

Miss Pepsi, at speed. Designed by Hacker, it was the last of the great traditional planing racers, a type that gave way to three-point racing boats. Courtesy Dossin Great Lakes Museum, Detroit

Hacker was nervous and tense. Bolger attributed this to the pressure of completing the design for what he considered the most important boat that he had done so far. He was preoccupied with that design. He would worry at night and then come into the office next morning and add a set of intermediate frames or make some other change. Jim Eddy, the project manager who was keeping exact records, would have to calculate his figures all over again.

In the late 1940s or early 1950s, John L. Hacker moved his office from Jefferson Avenue to the Kerr Building on Beaubien, also of course in Detroit. Evidently he was more prosperous, for at this office he hired a secretary.

At about this same time, Hacker was designing the last *Rainbow,* a cruiser for Harry Greening, who came into the office occasionally while the design was progressing. *Rainbow XI* was launched in 1952. It was 42 feet long and was built with a raised deck fore and aft; portholes in the side of the vessel provided light and ventilation. Hacker's eye for a handsome boat was shown by the attractiveness of what, with a raised deck all around, could have been an ugly looking ark. There was a semiopen bridge deck

that could be enclosed by a folding canvas top and curtains held on sail tracks. Driven by two Scripps engines of 110 horsepower each, it could make a maximum speed of about 12 miles per hour—quite a change for a boat named *Rainbow.* But according to Greening it was "by long odds the most comfortable and seaworthy boat I have owned to date."

Hacker was also designing a cruiser for another Canadian customer, this one a stock boat for the Gulf & Lake Navigation Co. Limited, of Montreal. A 67-footer driven by twin GM diesels through a V-drive, it was advertised in *Yachting* in October 1953. "Promenade Deck Diesel Powered Cruiser. Constructed under the supervision of John L. Hacker, N.A. to the highest specifications." The list of features was lengthy. Finally the advertisement promised "November delivery in New York."

He had recently designed two of the best-remembered racing boats. They were the last, most powerful of the classic hydroplane type—boats still remembered and discussed among racing enthusiasts. He had designed the finest runabouts, which continue to be revered. Yet, Bolger notes, Hacker seemed to be proudest of the "sea cruisers," as he called them, that he had

A Hacker 67-footer, *Huberton* was built in Lunenburg, Nova Scotia, in 1953 for a Halifax owner. Here the builders make the final adjustments on the boat. Note the touch of art deco trim at the bow. *The Mariners' Museum, Newport News, Virginia.*

Mercury, a 70-foot
Hacker cruiser built
in 1959 by the
Quincy Adams Yacht
Yard in Quincy,
Massachusetts. It
was powered by two
300-horsepower six-
cylinder GM
engines. Its cruising
speed was 17 miles
per hour, and its top
speed was 21.
*The Mariners'
Museum, Newport
News, Virginia*

designed. They were not as well known as his other work, but they were equally fine. "His displacement and moderate-speed cruisers were consistently ahead of their time and exceptionally handsome."

In 1952 John Hacker and his wife, Bertha, celebrated their 50th wedding anniversary, which was duly reported in the *Detroit News*. Though he and she had their differences, this was a family celebration of the kind that Hacker enjoyed:

"Congratulations on their Golden Wedding anniversary were being received today by Mr. and Mrs. John L. Hacker, of 14982 Kilbourne, native Detroiters who were married here. The anniversary was celebrated by a dinner at the Whittier Hotel, followed by a reception at the home of a nephew, Charles Hacker, of 931 Ashland."

Parting Company

The original Hacker Boat Company continued to operate, offering Hackercraft for sale. By then some of its boats were no longer designed by the master. What caused the final break is not known; perhaps he no longer thought it worthwhile to design for them; perhaps they had come to think of him as an outdated old fogy whose designs were no longer in style. The 1956 price list showed a 23-foot Overnighter express cruiser, an 18-foot Falcon utility (made of plywood), and 20-, 23-, and 26-foot "custom utilities," plus a 26-foot "custom runabout." The term "custom" probably meant that although they were standard designs they were built only to order. Chris-Craft had begun to make boats with flat sides, little tumble home aft, nearly rectangular transoms, and a minimum of flare at the bow, and the McCready company retained a different architect who followed this lead. It was the ultimate irony—Hackercraft now was copying Chris-Craft.

But the new boats were not popular. They had little individuality. If a buyer wanted a boat that looked like a Chris-Craft he would buy a Chris-Craft. The company still attempted to keep its "craftsman labor" as opposed to mass production, but growing labor costs in Detroit—one of the reasons that even the mass-producing Chris-Craft left the area that same year—plus the lingering financial burden of the canceled Korean War navy contract, S. Dudley McCready's increasing age, and the poor sales of unpopular boats all finally led the company to close its doors in 1957.

The relative positions of Hacker and his former company were well reflected in the advertising sections of the magazine *Boats* in January 1956, a year before the McCready-owned company gave up the ghost. On page 209 was a quarter-page advertisement for the Hacker Boat Company with a photo of its 23-foot Overnighter, which was not a Hacker design: "Swift-Seaworthy-Luxurious. The newest Hackercraft is built to custom standards." On page 220 of the same magazine there was another quarter-page ad showing a drawing of a large cruiser: "Build a Hacker for 1956. Many late stock designs up to 70 foot." In large letters at the bottom of the advertisement was "JOHN L. HACKER, N. A." and in smaller but quite evident letters "Not associated with Hacker Boat Co."

But John L. Hacker had the satisfaction of seeing the Hacker Boat Company come to its end in the following year.

That released him from his agreement to design stock runabouts and utilities only for the company. In the late 1950s the Gage Marine Corporation on Lake Geneva, Wisconsin, asked Hacker to design two boats for it. Older Hackercraft had given good service on the lake, both riding well and standing up to rough usage as excursion boats. Fiberglass boats were coming in, and it was hard to get good wooden designs, which Gage preferred. Hacker designed a 22-footer and a 26-footer. They came both as utilities and as runabouts. Over the years Gage built more than 25 of these Gage-Hackers, as they became known.

In 1959 or 1960 the Kerr Building, where Hacker had his office, was to be demolished to make room for a new freeway. He moved to a building at East Jefferson and Lakeview Avenues,

where he shared offices with his youngest brother, George, and with Nils Lucander, a naval architect who specialized in sailboats.

George, in a letter to John A. Hacker, John L.'s son, noted that the elder Hacker, now in his 80s, resented the fact that he could not work as hard or as long as he once had. "Not many years back he could work on the board for hours and not feel it, [but] he now works minutes or half hour and he is pooped and hits the chair, and, frankly I think that condition just irks him." For a man who not long ago gloried in the number of push-ups he could do, old age was frustrating. Even so, things were getting done. "Your Dad has the 70-footer to finish, and a 60 for the Montreal people awaiting his orders."

In 1959, the second year of its existence, the Detroit Powerboat Hall of Fame inducted John L. Hacker, saying "Hacker's contributions started more than 50 years ago as a designer and builder of race boats," and going on to list the main accomplishments. The following year the American Powerboat Association, meeting in Baton Rouge, Louisiana, named him a member of its honor squadron.

During these years some of Hacker's friends tried to prevail on the University of Michigan to give him an honorary degree or to recognize his accomplishments in some appropriate way. But he was not in a position to be a big donor. And back when Hacker first started to put "N. A." after his name, a naval architect did not need an academic blessing before he went to work. Hacker's lack of a university degree apparently left him outside the modern club, and his success may have been seen almost as an insult to it. The academic engineers appeared to view him much as a medical college would look at a self-trained healer. He never received university recognition, which perhaps says more about the university than about him.

On Saturday, February 25, 1961, John Hacker, as usual, had been working at his office on the weekend. When he came home that evening his daughter Marion and her husband were visiting. She describes events: "Suddenly he came up to me, took my hands into his, and with the sweetest smile said, 'I love you.' Moments later he was stricken, and speechless, and lived only five more days."

Phil Bolger: "He was an artist of a high order; everything he did had style. He himself was not a 'character'; it was his work that was flamboyant."

Postscript

The name Hacker Boat Company and the Hackercraft trademark passed through several hands and finally in the 1970s became the property of Bill Morgan, boat racer, boat restorer—and now boatbuilder and designer.

Before starting to build his own Hackercraft, Morgan restored over 50 old Hacker boats and came to know them intimately. But Hacker boats were never as numerous as some other brands, old boats that have survived are relatively scarce, and he eventually ran out of boats to restore. Then he decided to build new Hackers, though the old jigs and tools were long gone, and he had to make new patterns from the restored boats.

Although he believes that Hacker boats were the best that were built during the heyday of wooden runabouts, Morgan discovered what he considered the weaknesses of the old boats while doing restoration, and decided that they could be improved. So after building a few exact replicas, he began to add more frames and floor timbers, and to use additional bolts. Hacker enthusiasts might raise an eyebrow but the old boats had some noticeable flex; the new ones have none.

Undoubtedly if John L. Hacker were working today he would be using the technology of today. Like Morgan, he would be using the epoxy-saturated floor timbers, today's more powerful engines with stronger supports, and stainless steel fittings instead of chrome.

Although the old Hackercraft were known for their level ride, Morgan felt that their bows rose too high at top speed, so—some would call it lese majesty —he adjusted the bottom shape. At any speed the boats run level. Most of them look exactly like the old Hackercraft above the water, but the design is altered below the waterline.

Today vinyl upholstery has replaced the leather unless a new owner insists on the traditional seat covering. Vinyl better resists water, especially salt water, and the normal wear and tear of use—people stepping down from the dock or climbing over seats wearing their boat shoes, or dumping heavy objects onto the seats. Windshields are laminated and come in traditional or updated forms.

Stock runabouts and utilities run from 21 feet to 35 feet. Race boats run from 21 feet to 28 feet. Some are adaptations of Hacker's original designs; some are new designs in the Hacker idiom. Probably almost anything in custom boats is available if you should want a new *Lockpat.*

A recent unusual model that Morgan designed and refers to as a sport boat has a large aft cockpit, minimal tumble home aft, and a wide transom that slants outward and downward from the gunwale to the water. This last feature was seen on Hacker's *Au Revoir* of 1903 and no doubt on some of his later boats—he tried almost every combination over the years—but not on his classic runabouts or his later utilities. In this case it allows a swimming ladder to slant upward from the waterline at the stern to the deck just behind the big cockpit. Obviously swimming parties in relatively quiet places were foremost in Morgan's mind when he conceived this one. It is a wonderful accessory for a summer cottage. One would choose some other model—perhaps the 30-foot classic runabout—for use in unprotected waters on a rough day with a heavy following sea.

Today's Morgan Hackers are solidly built. All fastenings are stainless steel. Framing is oak. Sides are made of two layers of epoxy-saturated Honduras mahogany, for a total thickness of 3/4 inch. The bottoms are made of three layers bonded together with epoxy, for a total thickness of an inch, and Morgan has been known to pound a hammer on an outer layer to show that it leaves no impact marks. He tells of one owner who, somewhat under the influence, ran his 24-foot boat head-on into a dock at 30 miles an hour. The engine broke loose and slid forward, pulling the exhaust pipes out of the transom; the steering column was bent and the nosepiece was shredded, but other than that the boat didn't sustain any structural damage. The owner was unhurt, and possibly sobered. A fiberglass boat would probably have shattered, and so might its driver.

Morgan is one of several builders who build wooden craft using modern techniques. He specializes in Hackers; others have different concerns. Interest in such craft has grown in recent years, but still is tiny compared to the market for fiberglass boats. Woods today do not require as much care as their ancestors, but they still need more affectionate treatment than their fiberglass equivalents. On the other hand, a fiberglass boat depreciates almost as quickly as a car, while the value of a well-kept wooden boat is retained and may even increase.

If Hacker were here, he would not be standing still in a museum. He would be developing his ideas, designing specialized boats, moving ahead. His boats, like these, would be much easier and cheaper to care for than wooden boats of the past.

Wooden boatbuilding lives on, and so does the Hacker spirit.

NOTES AND BIBLIOGRAPHY

NOTES

Chapter 1

John L. Hacker's early years are described in Clarke. The biography of John F. Hacker, the boat designer's father, is in a newspaper clipping (showing neither source nor date) in the Reading Room File, Burton Historical Collection, Detroit Main Library. John F. stepped in front of a car and was killed in December 1921; see *Detroit News*, December 5, 1921, Part Two. "*Au Revoir*, a new Speed Launch on Detroit River," *Sail and Sweep*, November 1903 tells of that boat. The quotation from Gar Wood is in Brennan. An advertising pamphlet, ca.1914, *Van Blerck Marine Motors*, tells of the *Kitty Hawks, Oregon Kid, Stroller, Cloverleaf,* and *Jovial,* all Hacker boats with Van Blerck engines. The racing adventures of *Oregon Kid* come from *Pacific Motor Boat* issues in 1913 and 1914 and from Bashford, James, "Astoria Holds Another Great Regatta," *Motor Boat*, September 25, 1915. "The Chicago Water Carnival," *Yachting*, September 1912, tells of the burning of *Kitty Hawk.* "*Hawkeye* Wins Thousand Islands Cup," *The Rudder*, September 1916, tells of that event. The description of *Miss Miami* is from an advertisement in *Motor Boating*, September 1917. Chapman, Charles F., "*Detroit III* Wins the Gold Cup," *Motor Boating*, October 1918. [Notes that *Miss Miami* engine went into *Miss Detroit III*.] Much of the early material depends on Brennan, Gribbins, and Robinson. The extracts from A. W. MacKerer's letters were provided by his son, Don MacKerer. Hacker's daughter, Marion Hurst, has given much background information.

Chapter 2

Sources not in the text are either from boating publications of the time or the following references. Hacker's 1919 purchase of Mt. Clemens property is reported both in the *Detroit News* for October 18 and the *Mount Clemens Monitor* for October 24. The names of the initial officers in the 1920 company are in the 1920–1921 *Detroit City Directory.* Fostle notes the similarity between the 1920s Bear Cats and Hacker's designs. Lindquist tells of the boats designed for Richardson. The 1925 date of S. D. McCready's joining the company (and a photo of him around which the material is organized) is in the *Pageant of Progress* for Macomb County, Michigan, published in July 1928 by the Nellis Newspapers (in Mt. Clemens Public Library). The Mt. Clemens *City Directory* also shows McCready first a resident of that city in 1925. Hacker production figure of three a week in early 1925 appeared on page 27 of the May 25 *Motor Boat* of that year.

The figures for 1928 are in the Mount Clemens *Daily Leader* of August 18. Material on Chris-Craft is from Rodengen. The extract from A. W. MacKerrer's letter was provided by his son, Doug MacKerer. Material on Gar Wood is from Mollica. The Liggett cruiser is described in *Motor Boat* for January 10 and November 10, 1925. The cruiser built by Sterney Woodcraft is in the July 25 and August 15, 1926, *Motor Boat*. Ronald Lane has contributed much information about his 55-foot cruiser *Bo-Peep II* and the Hacker-Fermann relationship. Races in Germany and Italy are reported in Hacker ads in *Yachting* of August 1930 and *Motor Boating* of December 1930, and in a news item in *Motor Boating* of September 1931. The Egyptian account is under the heading "Yard and Shop" in the January 1930 *Motor Boating*. Hacker output in 1930 was estimated by Tom Flood, Hacker historian.

The account of the Hacker connection with the Century Boat Company is from documents quoted in the text and from Paul Miklos, Century historian. Century's bankruptcy story is from Wittig, whose detailed company history from that time forward makes it clear that Hacker was not involved in later Century operations. Duke and Gray, and Gray and Du Vernet tell about the Muskoka boats. S. Steven McCready provided internal company documents quoted and the schedule of plant expansion. Hacker's altering of stock boats on seeing the shapes of their purchasers is told by Tom Flood. The departure of Van Blerck from his own company is noted in *Motor Boat* for December 1930. The story of the Pfeiffelman boat is under "Yard and Shop" in the July 1930 *Motor Boating*. The Corps of Engineers purchase is in the June 1931 issue. "On the Lake of the Ozarks" in the October 1931 *Motor Boating* tells of the Union Land and Development Company's purchase of Hacker boats.

Chapter 3

The large custom runabouts that preceded *Lockpat II* are described in *Motor Boat* for December 10, 1923, and December 10, 1926. Information about that boat at the Harmsworth Races is in an advertisement in the December 1931 *Motor Boating*. The cruiser *Skylark II* is described in *Motor Boat* for September 10, 1923. The cruiser *Rosewill* is described by Moore. The horsepower of the Packard engine in the king of Siam's boat was given in the October 1930 *Motor Boat*. The transaction in gold bullion to pay for the boat is told in a piece by Steve Saph Sr., in the 1999 Mount Clemens Boat Show Program.

Chapter 4

Major sources on *El Lagarto* are Crook, W. Melvin. "The Lady With a Past," *Yachting*, July 1956; Morris, Everett B., "Salute to Champions," *Motor Boating*, February 1936; and Rooney, Andrew A., "Cinderella Speedboat," *Motor Boating*, March 1949. Most of the racing descriptions are drawn from reports that are cited in the text. Any uncited details are from the boating magazines of the day. More complete technical descriptions of *Rainbow II* and its development can be found in *Motor Boat* for September 25, 1923, and January 10, 1924. The Griffin race account is much longer than the quoted abstract and should be read by anyone interested in the Gold Cup races of that time. Letters to Edsel Ford suggesting new Gold Cup racers and from Ford turning down the ideas are in the collections of the Henry Ford Museum & Greenfield Village. The racing story of the *Little Miss Canadas* is told by Wilson.

Chapter 5

The account of Hacker's turning in his stock is in company records provided by S. Steven McCready, as is the agreement permitting Hacker thereafter to design only limited types of boats. McCready also provided the navy report comparing various makes of boats. Brennan and Gribbins cover this period. The description of Gold Cup racing conditions is from Crook. The Wilson racing account is in Wilson's book. Other racing material is from the boating magazines of the corresponding years. Pearson, Bob, "Mahogany Muscle," *Lakeland Boating*, March 2001 tells of the radio-controlled boats.

Marion Hacker Hurst has provided many details. Hacker historian Tom Flood, whose father, Leo Flood, was Hacker purchasing agent from 1925 to 1957, and who himself worked in the plant for a few years as a youngster, believes that S. Dudley McCready wanted full control of the company, which led to Hacker's removal.

Chapter 6

Hacker's office has been described by Nelson Zimmer. The Wangards cover *Pardon Me* in detail. Descriptions of races are from the boating press of the day. Personal recollections are from Hacker's daughter, Marion Hurst, and from Phil Bolger, Jay Ottinger, and Nelson Zimmer. Developments in the McCready's Hacker Boat Company are from Tom Flood and from published material cited in the text. Flood has given the number of boats per month and the number of employees of the Hacker Boat Company in the early 1950s. He also believes that McCready's need to personally control all aspects of the company kept it from growing, and contributed to its general decline.

The Staudacher quotation is from the *Unlimited NewsJournal*, October 1986. The unbuilt Hacker designs for Dodge are described in the *Unlimited NewsJournal* February 2000. Information on the Muskoka boats comes from Duke and Gray, and from Gray and Du Vernet. *Rainbow XI* is described in *Motor Boating*, February 1953. The Gage-Hacker is covered by Speltz, vol. 2. Hacker's entry into the Hall of Fame is described by the Detroit press of the day. Attempts to get an honorary degree for Hacker are described in *Lakeland Boating's* "Salute: John L. Hacker."

S. Dudley McCready Sr. died on March 28, 1980; the obituary was in the *Macomb [County] Daily*, a local Michigan paper.

Bibliography

Brennan, Walter K. "John L. Hacker, Dean of Yacht Designers." *Motor Boating*, December 1959.

Chapman, Charles F. "Motor Boat Racing Past Present and Future." *Motor Boating*, November 1919.

Clarke, S. J. *The City of Detroit, Michigan, 1701–1922.* Vol. 5. Detroit: The S. J. Clarke Publishing Company, 1922. [Early Hacker biography.]

Cook, Patrick. "Lake Success: Hacker Boats." *Forbes*, September 23, 1996. [Present-day Hacker Boat Co.]

Crook, W. Melvin. "The First 55 Years." *Yachting*, July 1959. [History of the Gold Cup races and boats to that time.]

Desmond, Charles. *Naval Architecture Simplified.* New York: Rudder Publishing Company, 1935. [Hacker convex bows.]

Doane, Arthur E. "Ten Years of Runabout Progress." *Motor Boat,* June 1931.

Duke, A. H. and Gray, W. M. *The Boatbuilders of Muskoka.* Toronto: Boston Mills Press, Stoddart, 1985.

Fostle, D. W. *Speedboat.* Mystic, CT: Mystic Seaport Museum Stores, 1988.

Gribbins, Joseph. "Hacker and His Craft." *Nautical Quarterly,* Summer 1981.

Gray, William M. and Du Vernet, Timothy C. *Wood & Glory.* Toronto: Boston Mills Press, Stoddart, 1997. [Muskoka boats.]

Griffin, Charles F. "A Contestant's Impression of the President's Cup Race." *Motor Boating*, November 1934.

"Hacker Boat Company." *Classic Boating,* July/August 1989. [The present-day company.]

"The Hacker Phenomenon." *Motor Boat,* April 10, 1929.

Hagan, Michael. "The Heritage of Edward II." *Classic Boating,* May/June 2000.

Huber, Bob. "John Hacker Remembered." *Classic Boating,* July/August 1996. [An interview with Tom Flood, who knew Hacker and his company.]

Lindquist, William C. *The Richardson Story.* Rochester, NY: privately published, n.d.

"Many Newly Built Runabouts Are An Indication of Boating as Usual." *Motor Boating,* January 1918.

Mollica, Anthony S. Jr. *Gar Wood Boats.* Osceola, WI: MBI Publishing Company, 1999.

Moore, C. Philip. *Yachts in a Hurry.* New York: W.W. Norton and Company, n.d.

Mount Clemens Antique and Classic Boat Show. 1999 Program.

Mount Clemens, Michigan, Public Library Paper. "Hacker Boat Company," n.d.

Neal, Robert J. *Packards at Speed.* Kent, Washington: Aero-Marine History Publishing Company, 1995.

Nutting, William Washburn. "Single-Handing It Among the Shops." *Motor Boat,* August 10, 1914. [Van Blerck's engine shop, *Hawkeye*]

Robinson, John G. " Evolution of the Runabout." *Motor Boating,* January 1940.

Rodengen, Jeffrey L. *The Legend of Chris-Craft.* Fort Lauderdale, Florida: Write Stuff Syndicate, 1993.

"Salute: John L. Hacker." *Lakeland Boating,* June 1959.

Wangard, Norm and Jim. *Classic Powercraft.* 2 vols. Oconomowoc, Wisconsin: Classic Powercraft, 1986.

Weir, Lynne B. and York, Grace. *Historic and Architectural Reconnaissance Survey.* Mount Clemens: City of Mount Clemens, 1992.

Wilson, Harold. *Boats Unlimited.* Erin, Ontario: Boston Mills Press, 1990. [Wilson racing with Hacker boats.]

Wittig, William G. *The Story of the Century.* Manistee, Michigan: The Century Boat Company, 1984.

The four speedboat scrapbooks compiled by William T. Campbell are of great help in researching Hacker's racing boats.

Index